Mastering Pickling & Fermentation

A Prepper's Guide to Preserving Food

Emma Clarkson

Table of Contents

INTRODUCTION

"Mastering Pickling & Fermentation: A Prepper's Guide to Preserving Food" is an essential resource for anyone looking to delve into the world of food preservation through traditional methods. This comprehensive guide offers a unique blend of practical advice, historical context, and modern applications, mainly focusing on the needs of preppers and those interested in sustainable living. The book begins by exploring the rich history of pickling and fermentation, illustrating how these methods have been vital for survival and culinary delight across various cultures and epochs. It then transitions into the science behind these processes, demystifying how natural bacteria and brine can transform everyday foods' shelf life and flavor.

The book's heart lies in its extensive, step-by-step tutorials and recipes, designed for beginners and experts alike. From classic dill pickles and sauerkraut to exotic kimchi and kombucha, the reader is taken on a flavorful journey, learning how to harness the power of natural fermentation to not only extend the life of their food but also to enhance its nutritional value and taste. The guide also addresses safety practices, troubleshooting common issues, and tips for storage and long-term planning, making it an indispensable tool for preppers and homesteaders.

"Mastering Pickling & Fermentation" is more than just a recipe book; it's a survival manual and a testament to the resilience and ingenuity of human food practices. Whether you're preparing for uncertain times or simply eager to explore the world of fermented foods, this book is a must-have on your shelf.

CHAPTER I

Getting Started with Pickling

The Basics of Pickling

Pickling, a method steeped in history, is not just a culinary technique but a bridge between the past and present, connecting us to a time when preserving food was vital for survival. The basics of pickling are both an art and a science, rooted in the need to extend the shelf life of perishable food items, particularly in regions and eras without modern refrigeration. This section delves into the fundamental aspects of pickling, exploring its history, processes, and the cultural significance it holds in various societies.

The history of pickling dates back thousands of years, with records indicating its presence in ancient civilizations like Mesopotamia. Originally, pickling started as a necessity to preserve food, especially for long journeys and harsh winters. Soldiers, travelers, and sailors relied on pickled foods for sustenance. Over time, pickling evolved beyond a mere survival tactic to become a culinary tradition in many cultures, each developing its unique methods and flavors.

At its core, pickling involves preserving food by anaerobic fermentation in brine or immersion in vinegar. The primary goal is to extend the food's shelf life by creating an environment hostile to microbial growth. Two main methods of pickling are recognized: vinegar-based pickling and fermentation-based pickling. Vinegar-based pickling, also known as quick pickling, involves submerging food in a solution of vinegar, water, and salt, often with various seasonings for flavor. This method does not involve fermentation and can be prepared in a relatively short amount of time. In contrast, fermentation-based pickling relies on the natural bacteria present in the food, particularly lactic acid bacteria, to ferment the food. This process not only preserves the food but also enhances its nutritional value and can contribute to gut health due to the presence of probiotics.

The science of pickling is fascinating. In fermentation pickling, the process begins with the submersion of the food item, commonly vegetables, in a brine solution. The salt in the brine inhibits the growth of harmful bacteria while allowing the beneficial lactic acid bacteria to thrive. These bacteria convert sugars in the food into lactic acid, which acts as a natural preservative. Thus, The acidic environment prevents the growth of spoilage-causing microorganisms, effectively preserving the food. In vinegar pickling, the acetic acid in vinegar performs a similar function, creating an environment that prevents microbial growth.

Pickled foods are preserved for more extended periods and undergo a transformation in flavor and texture. The pickling process can impart a range of flavors, from sour to spicy, and can also result in a pleasing crunchiness in the food. This transformation has led to the popularity of pickled foods in various culinary traditions worldwide. For instance, in Eastern Europe, pickled cucumbers and cabbage are staple foods, while in Asia, pickled vegetables like kimchi are a part of daily meals.

The cultural significance of pickling cannot be understated. Pickled foods are associated with traditional festivities and family gatherings in many cultures. Recipes for pickled foods are often passed down through generations, carrying with them stories and memories. Additionally, pickling has seen a resurgence in recent years, particularly in the context of sustainable living and the farm-to-table movement. Home pickling has become popular as a way to reduce food waste and maintain a connection with the food we consume.

In conclusion, the basics of pickling encompass a rich tapestry of history, science, and culture. From its origins as a means of survival to its current status as a cherished culinary practice, pickling has stood the test of time. It represents a harmonious blend of necessity and flavor, a testament to human ingenuity in food preservation. Whether it is the quick tang of a vinegar-pickled cucumber or the complex flavors of fermented kimchi, pickled foods offer a unique taste experience while reminding us of our connection to the past and our continued journey in the culinary world. As we look to more sustainable and health-conscious ways of living, the art and science of pickling stand out as both a practical skill and a cultural heritage worth preserving.

Equipment and Supplies Needed

The journey into the world of pickling and fermentation is a culinary adventure and a practice steeped in tradition and practicality. One must be equipped with the right tools and supplies to embark on this journey. This section explores the essential equipment and supplies needed for pickling and fermentation, delving into their purposes, varieties, and the nuances of selecting the right items to ensure safety and success in these age-old food preservation techniques.

First and foremost, the cornerstone of any pickling endeavor is the container where the pickling process occurs. Glass jars, particularly Mason jars, are widely favored for their non-reactive nature and the airtight seal they provide. The use of glass allows for easy monitoring of the pickling process, and the material does not interact with acids or salts, ensuring that the flavors of the pickled items remain unaltered. For larger batches, ceramic crocks or food-grade plastic containers can be used, especially for fermentation pickling, where larger volumes are often processed. It is crucial to ensure that these containers are free from cracks and chips to maintain a clean and safe environment for food preservation.

Lids and weights play a significant role in the fermentation process. Airlock lids, which allow gases produced during fermentation to escape while preventing air from entering, are invaluable for creating an anaerobic environment essential for successful fermentation. Similarly, weights are used to submerge the food in brine, avoiding exposure to air, which can lead to spoilage or mold growth. These weights can be specialized fermentation weights or clean, boiled stones; the key is that they must be non-reactive and heavy enough to maintain submersion.

The choice of salt is another critical factor in pickling and fermentation. It's essential to use pickling or canning salt, as these are free from additives like iodine or anti-caking agents that can cloud brine or inhibit fermentation. The purity of the salt ensures that the chemical balance needed for successful pickling and fermentation is maintained. Likewise, when vinegar is required, especially in quick pickling, it's important to use vinegar with sufficient acidity (typically 5% or higher), such as apple cider vinegar or white distilled vinegar, for effective preservation.

Measuring tools, such as measuring cups and spoons, are indispensable for ensuring the correct ratios of salt, water, and vinegar. Precision is vital in pickling and fermentation to achieve the desired taste and ensure food safety. A kitchen scale can also be beneficial, particularly for fermentation, where the ratio of salt to vegetables can be critical.

Utensils like wooden spoons, ladles, and tongs are necessary for handling ingredients and preparing brines.

Using non-reactive utensils is vital to avoid any chemical reaction with acidic ingredients. Additionally, a wide-mouth funnel can be particularly useful for transferring brine and vegetables into jars, minimizing spills and keeping the workspace clean.

A pH meter or test strips can be a valuable tool for those delving into fermentation. Monitoring the acidity level is crucial for ensuring a safe fermentation process. A successful ferment should have a pH level of 4.6 or lower, inhibiting harmful bacteria growth.

Lastly, cleanliness is paramount in pickling and fermentation. All equipment must be thoroughly cleaned and sterilized before use. This can be done by boiling the tools or using a dishwasher with a sanitizing cycle. This step is crucial to avoid contamination and ensure the safety of the preserved food.

In conclusion, pickling and fermentation requires more than just culinary skills; it demands the right set of tools and supplies. From the choice of containers to the selection of salts and vinegars, each element plays a vital role in the success of the preservation process. Understanding and assembling these tools and supplies is the first step in transforming fresh produce into flavorful, preserved foods. Whether a novice or an experienced practitioner, having the proper equipment is key to mastering the techniques of pickling and fermentation, ensuring not only delightful flavors but also the safety and longevity of the preserved foods. This collection of equipment and supplies forms the foundation upon which the rich and diverse world of pickling and fermentation is built, offering an avenue to explore culinary traditions, embrace sustainable living, and enjoy the timeless practice of food preservation.

Selection of Fruits and Vegetables for Pickling

The art of pickling, a culinary practice rich in tradition and innovation, hinges significantly on selecting fruits and vegetables. This choice is not merely a matter of taste but also of understanding the intricate dance between the produce, the pickling brine, and the fermentation process. This section explores the various aspects of selecting fruits and vegetables for pickling, considering factors such as seasonality, freshness, texture, and flavor profile.

At the heart of successful pickling lies the principle of using the freshest produce available. Freshness is paramount because it determines the final pickled product's crunchiness, flavor, and overall quality. Vegetables and fruits used for pickling should be ripe but still firm, free from bruises or soft spots, which could compromise the texture and potentially lead to spoilage. Seasonality plays a crucial role in this regard. Pickling what is in season ensures optimal freshness and supports sustainable practices by reducing food miles and promoting local produce.

In terms of vegetables, cucumbers are perhaps the most iconic choice for pickling, but the world of pickling vegetables extends far beyond. Root vegetables like carrots, radishes, and beets offer a delightful crunch and a vibrant palette of colors that enhance the visual appeal of pickled assortments. Cruciferous vegetables like cauliflower and cabbage are excellent for fermentation, as their dense structure holds up well in brine over time. Green beans, asparagus, and even okra can be transformed through pickling, each with unique texture and flavor. It is essential to consider the individual characteristics of these vegetables, as some may require blanching or slicing to ensure even pickling and flavor absorption.

Though less common in the pickling world, fruits offer a delightful contrast of flavors. Fruits like apples, pears, and peaches can be pickled, often with the addition of spices like cinnamon or cloves to complement their natural sweetness. Berries can also be pickled, though they require a gentle hand due to their delicate nature. The use of fruits in pickling extends the culinary possibilities, allowing for a blend of sweet, sour, and tangy flavors that can elevate dishes or be enjoyed as unique condiments.

Preparing fruits and vegetables for pickling is as crucial as their selection. Washing the produce thoroughly to remove any dirt or chemicals is a given. However, care must be taken not to over-soak vegetables, as this can lead to a loss of crunch. Peeling is optional and often a matter of personal preference or based on a specific recipe. Some vegetables, like cucumbers, may benefit from trimming their ends, as they can contain enzymes that soften them. Cutting the produce into uniform sizes ensures even pickling and fermentation, making for a more consistent end product.

Another aspect to consider is the natural flavor profile of the fruits and vegetables chosen. This plays a significant role in determining the types of spices and herbs that can be added to the pickling mix. For instance, dill and garlic are classic pairings with cucumbers, while beets may be paired with flavors like mustard seeds and peppercorns. Understanding these flavor affinities can significantly enhance the pickling experience, allowing for creative and personalized pickling adventures.

It's also worth noting that while most fruits and vegetables can be pickled, some are better suited for this process than others. High-water-content vegetables, for example, might become too soggy when pickled. Experimentation can lead to delightful discoveries, but it's essential to understand how different produce will react in a pickling solution.

In conclusion, the selection of fruits and vegetables for pickling is a process that combines science, art, and a bit of personal flair. The freshest, seasonally appropriate produce will always yield the best results in flavor and texture. Understanding the unique characteristics of each fruit and vegetable, from their natural flavor profiles to their textural integrity, is vital to creating successful pickled products. Whether one is pickling for personal enjoyment, to preserve an abundant harvest, or to explore the depths of culinary creativity, the thoughtful selection of produce is the first and most crucial step. As pickling continues to enjoy a renaissance among home cooks and professional chefs alike, the endless possibilities of pickled fruits and vegetables are a testament to this enduring and ever-evolving art form.

Brine Recipes and Ratios

The art of pickling, which turns ordinary fruits and vegetables into tangy, zesty, and often crunchy delights, relies heavily on the brine. This simple yet intricate solution is the lifeline of the pickling process. In this section, we will delve into the world of brine recipes and ratios, exploring how different components interact to create a variety of flavors and textures in pickled produce.

The brine, at its most basic, is a mixture of water, salt, and often vinegar, with the addition of various herbs and spices to impart distinct flavors. The ratio of these ingredients plays a pivotal role in the success of the pickling process, affecting everything from taste to texture, and even the preservation quality of the final product.

Water is the foundation of the brine, acting as a solvent in which salt, vinegar, and other flavorings are dissolved. The quality of water used is crucial, as impurities or high mineral content can affect the pickling process and the final product's taste. Distilled or filtered water is often recommended to avoid these issues.

Salt is a key ingredient in brine, serving multiple purposes. It enhances flavor, helps maintain the crispness of the produce, and, in fermentative pickling, encourages the growth of desirable bacteria while inhibiting harmful ones. The type of salt used can vary - while pickling or kosher salt is commonly used due to its purity and lack of additives, other salts, like sea salt, can also be used for different flavor profiles. The salt concentration in the brine can vary depending on the recipe and the desired result, but a general rule of thumb for a basic brine is a ratio of 1 to 2 tablespoons of salt per quart of water.

Vinegar, another fundamental component of many brine solutions, adds acidity to the mix. The type of vinegar used can significantly influence the flavor of the pickled product. White vinegar, with its clean, sharp taste, is popular for its neutrality, while apple cider vinegar introduces a fruitier note. The acidity of vinegar not only flavors the produce but also plays a critical role in preservation, particularly in quick pickling methods where fermentation is not involved. The typical ratio for vinegar in brine is about one part vinegar to two parts water, but this can vary depending on the desired level of acidity and the specific recipe.

Adding sugar to the brine can balance the acidity and saltiness with a touch of sweetness. This is particularly common in pickles like bread-and-butter pickles, where a sweet flavor profile is desired. The amount of sugar can range from a teaspoon to several cups, depending on the recipe and personal preference.

Herbs and spices are what truly set one pickle apart from another. Common additions include dill, garlic, mustard seeds, peppercorns, cloves, and bay leaves, but the possibilities are virtually endless. These flavorings can be adjusted according to personal taste and the type of produce being pickled.

In fermentative pickling, where natural bacteria are relied upon to create acidity, the brine is typically simpler, often consisting of just water and salt. The salt concentration in this method is critical, as it needs to be sufficient to inhibit the growth of harmful bacteria, but not so high as to prevent the fermentation process. The ratios can vary, but a general guideline is a 2-5% salt concentration by weight.

It's important to note that brine ratios are not just about flavor. They also impact the safety and shelf life of the pickled product. A brine with insufficient acidity may not properly preserve the produce, leading to spoilage and potential health risks. Therefore, following tested recipes and guidelines, especially for beginners, is crucial.

In conclusion, the world of brine recipes and ratios is one of balance and experimentation. The right combination of water, salt, vinegar, sugar, and spices can transform simple produce into a complex and flavorful preserve. Understanding the basics of brine composition and the role of each ingredient is essential for any aspiring pickler. The journey begins with the brine, whether aiming for a crunchy dill pickle, a tangy kimchi, or a sweetly spiced fruit preserve. As with any culinary endeavor, mastering the brine takes practice and patience, but the reward is a world of flavors, textures, and preserved bounty that can be enjoyed year-round.

Traditional vs. Quick Pickling Methods

Pickling, an ancient culinary practice, has evolved over centuries into various techniques, each with its unique characteristics and results. Among these, traditional and quick pickling are the most commonly practiced methods. While sharing the basic principle of preserving food in an acidic medium, these methods differ significantly in terms of process, time frame, flavor development, and shelf life.

This section explores the nuances of traditional and quick pickling methods, shedding light on their historical backgrounds, processes, and the distinct qualities they impart to the pickled products.

Traditional pickling, often called fermentation pickling, is a method steeped in history, dating back thousands of years. This process relies on the natural fermentation of vegetables in a saltwater brine, a technique used by many cultures worldwide to preserve food. The key to this method is the natural lactic acid bacteria present on the surface of vegetables. When submerged in a saltwater solution, these bacteria convert sugars present in the food into lactic acid. This natural fermentation process not only preserves the vegetables but also enriches them with probiotics, beneficial for gut health.

The traditional pickling process is slow, typically taking several days to weeks, depending on the vegetable, salt concentration, and room temperature. As the vegetables ferment, they develop a distinctive sour flavor and can retain a crisp texture. The process requires monitoring and patience, as it involves ensuring that the vegetables remain submerged under the brine and that the environment is anaerobic to prevent spoilage. Traditional pickles are often celebrated for their complex flavors and health benefits, making them a favorite in many cultures.

On the other hand, quick pickling is a relatively modern method that offers a faster way to achieve similar, albeit not identical, results. This method, also known as vinegar pickling, involves immersing the vegetables in a solution of vinegar, water, salt, and sometimes sugar, along with various spices and herbs for flavoring. Unlike traditional pickling, quick pickling does not involve a fermentation process. Instead, the acidity of the vinegar acts as the preserving agent, inhibiting the growth of spoilage-causing microorganisms.

The quick pickling process can be completed in several hours, and the pickles are usually ready to eat once they have cooled down. This method is ideal for those who want to enjoy pickled vegetables without the long waiting period associated with traditional pickling. Quick pickles tend to have a sharper, more pronounced acidic flavor than traditionally fermented pickles' subtle sourness. However, they lack the probiotic benefits of fermented pickles since they do not undergo a natural fermentation process.

The choice between traditional and quick pickling often depends on the desired outcome and available time. Traditional pickling is preferred by those who appreciate fermented foods' depth of flavor and health benefits. It is a process that requires attention to detail, such as maintaining the correct salt concentration in the brine and ensuring a proper fermentation environment. Traditional pickles also have a longer shelf life when stored correctly, making them a practical choice for long-term preservation.

Quick pickling, with its simplicity and speed, is ideal for home cooks who want to add a tangy crunch to their meals without the lengthy fermentation process. This method allows for more immediate gratification and is versatile, as almost any vegetable can be quickly pickled. Quick pickles are typically stored in the refrigerator and have a shorter shelf life than traditional pickles.

In conclusion, traditional and quick pickling methods have a unique place in the culinary world. Traditional pickling, with its roots in ancient preservation techniques, offers a depth of flavor and health benefits that come with natural fermentation. It appeals to those who enjoy the art of slow food and the rich cultural heritage embodied in fermented pickles. On the other hand, quick pickling suits the modern, fast-paced lifestyle, providing a convenient way to add a zesty flavor to meals. Both methods highlight the versatility and creativity inherent in pickling, allowing cooks to experiment with flavors and techniques to preserve the seasons' bounty. Whether one chooses the time-honored tradition of fermentation or the speedy convenience of vinegar pickling, the world of pickled foods offers a delightful array of tastes and textures to explore.

CHAPTER II

Mastering the Art of Fermentation

Introduction to Fermentation

Fermentation, a process as ancient as civilization itself, has been a cornerstone in culinary and cultural practices worldwide. This section introduces the art and science of fermentation, exploring its history, biological basis, and diverse applications in food and beverage preparation.

The roots of fermentation trace back to the earliest human civilizations, where it likely emerged as a serendipitous discovery. Ancient people noticed that certain foods and beverages transformed when left in certain conditions, developing new flavors and textures, and often becoming more digestible and safer to consume. This process, driven by microorganisms, became a crucial method for food preservation, long before the advent of modern refrigeration. Across different cultures, fermentation has been used to produce a vast array of foods and beverages, from the cheese and yogurt of Europe to the kimchi of Korea, the sauerkraut of Germany, and the wines and beers found globally.

At its core, fermentation is a metabolic process in which microorganisms such as bacteria, yeast, or fungi convert organic compounds - often carbohydrates like sugars - into alcohol, acids, and gases. This biochemical transformation not only helps in preserving the food but also enhances its nutritional profile. For instance, lactic acid fermentation, seen in yogurt and sauerkraut, involves lactic acid bacteria converting sugars into lactic acid, a natural preservative that inhibits the growth of harmful bacteria. Similarly, in alcoholic fermentation, yeast converts sugars into ethanol and carbon dioxide, as seen in the production of beer and wine.

The magic of fermentation lies not just in preservation but also in the creation of new flavors, textures, and aromas. Fermented foods often develop a distinct tanginess and depth of flavor, along with potential health benefits. Many fermented foods are rich in probiotics, beneficial bacteria that can improve gut health. Additionally, fermentation can increase the bioavailability of nutrients, making fermented foods a valuable part of a balanced diet.

Fermentation can occur naturally, as it often does with wild fermentation where naturally occurring microbes are harnessed. However, it can also be a controlled process, where specific yeast or bacteria strains are introduced to achieve desired results, as seen in bread, beer, and cheese making. This control over the process allows for consistency in flavor and texture, which is crucial for commercial production.

Fermentation requires a basic understanding of the factors that influence microbial activity. Temperature, pH, salt concentration, and oxygen exposure are critical parameters that must be monitored and managed. For example, most lactic acid fermentation processes require an anaerobic (oxygen-free) environment, a certain temperature range, and specific salt concentrations to ensure the optimal growth of lactic acid bacteria.

The art of fermentation is not static; it is a dynamic field that has evolved over time. Traditional methods have been honed and adapted, and modern scientific understanding has expanded the possibilities of fermentation. Contemporary chefs and food enthusiasts are exploring novel ways to ferment foods, pushing the boundaries of flavor and texture. This exploration is not just limited to food but extends to beverages, where craft brewers and distillers are experimenting with different fermentation techniques to create unique alcoholic drinks.

In conclusion, fermentation is a fascinating blend of biology, chemistry, history, and art. It is a testament to human ingenuity and adaptability, a process that has allowed cultures to thrive by preserving food and enhancing its flavors and nutritional value. Whether it is the sharp tang of a fermented pickle, the creamy richness of yogurt, or the complex flavors of a fine wine, the influence of fermentation on our food and culture is undeniable. As we continue to explore the microbial world and its interactions with our food, the ancient practice of fermentation remains at the forefront of culinary innovation, offering endless possibilities for discovery and enjoyment.

The Science Behind Fermentation

Fermentation, a hallmark of human ingenuity in food preservation and preparation, is as much a scientific phenomenon as it is a culinary art. This section delves into the science behind fermentation, exploring the biochemical processes and the roles of microorganisms in transforming food at a molecular level.

At its core, fermentation is a metabolic process where microorganisms like bacteria, yeasts, and molds convert organic compounds, especially carbohydrates, into alcohol, gases, or acids. This biochemical reaction, primarily anaerobic (occurring in the absence of oxygen), has been harnessed throughout human history to preserve food, enhance its nutritional value, and develop unique flavors and textures. The science behind this transformative process is complex and fascinating, involving a delicate balance of factors such as microorganisms, temperature, pH, and substrate composition.

One of the most common forms of fermentation is lactic acid fermentation. This process is driven by lactic acid bacteria (LAB), such as Lactobacillus, which are naturally present in many foods and environments. LAB converts sugars like glucose, fructose, and sucrose into lactic acid. This acidification creates a hostile environment for harmful bacteria, thereby acting as a natural preservative. Lactic acid fermentation is responsible for the tangy taste of yogurt, the sourness of sauerkraut, and the distinctive flavor of sourdough bread. Beyond preservation, this process also enhances the digestibility of food and can increase the availability of vitamins and minerals.

Another significant type of fermentation is alcoholic fermentation, primarily carried out by yeasts, particularly Saccharomyces cerevisiae. In this process, yeasts metabolize sugars to produce ethanol and carbon dioxide. This form of fermentation is central to the production of alcoholic beverages such as beer, wine, and spirits, and is also a crucial step in the baking of leavened bread. The carbon dioxide produced during fermentation causes bread dough to rise, while the ethanol evaporates during baking.

Fermentation is also characterized by the production of secondary metabolites that contribute to fermented foods' unique flavors and aromas. These compounds include alcohols, esters, ketones, and phenols, each adding a distinct element to the sensory profile of the food. The exact composition of these metabolites can vary based on the specific strains of microorganisms involved, the fermentation conditions, and the substrate being fermented.

The conditions under which fermentation occurs are critical to the success of the process. Temperature, for instance, plays a vital role in regulating the activity of fermenting microorganisms. Most fermentative microbes thrive at specific temperature ranges, and deviations from these can alter the fermentation rate or the final product's quality. Similarly, the pH of the fermentation environment affects microbial growth and the fermentation pathway. Many fermented foods start at a neutral or slightly acidic pH, with the environment becoming more acidic as fermentation progresses, due to the production of organic acids.

Salt concentration is another critical factor, especially in lactic acid fermentation. Salt inhibits the growth of unwanted microorganisms while allowing salt-tolerant LAB to thrive. This selective inhibition is crucial in the initial stages of fermentation, ensuring that the desired bacteria dominate the microbial ecosystem.

In recent years, the science of fermentation has expanded beyond traditional methods, incorporating modern biotechnology to enhance and control the fermentation process. Advances in molecular biology and microbiology have led to the development of starter cultures with specific properties, enabling more consistent and targeted fermentation processes. These innovations have opened up new possibilities in food production, allowing for the creation of novel flavors and textures, as well as improved health benefits.

In conclusion, the science behind fermentation is a remarkable blend of biology, chemistry, and physics. It involves harnessing the power of microorganisms to transform food in ways that preserve it, make it more nutritious, and enhance its flavors and textures. The process of fermentation is a testament to the symbiotic relationship between humans and microorganisms, a relationship that has been cultivated and refined over centuries. As we unravel the complexities of microbial ecosystems and their metabolic pathways, fermentation science holds immense potential for innovation in food science, nutrition, and gastronomy.

Equipment and Supplies for Fermentation

Fermentation, an age-old process harnessed to preserve and enhance the flavor of foods, requires skill and knowledge and specific equipment and supplies. These tools are crucial in creating the right environment for beneficial microorganisms to thrive and ferment. This section delves into the various equipment and supplies essential for fermentation, their purposes, and their role in ensuring successful fermentation projects.

At the core of fermentation equipment is the fermentation vessel. The choice of vessel is pivotal, as it needs to provide an appropriate environment for fermentation while preventing contamination. Glass jars are a popular choice due to their non-reactive nature and transparency, which allows for easy monitoring of the fermentation process. Food-grade plastic containers are also used, especially for larger batches, as they are lightweight and durable. However, ensuring they are free from BPA and other chemicals that might leach into the food is critical. Traditionalists might opt for ceramic crocks, which have been used for centuries in various cultures for fermenting vegetables. These crocks often come with weights to submerge the food and a water seal to allow gases to escape while keeping air out.

The use of weights in fermentation keeps the food submerged in the brine, creating an anaerobic (oxygen-free) environment crucial for many types of fermentation. Weights can be made of glass, ceramic, or food-grade plastic. Some fermenters use clean, boiled stones as weights. The key is that they must be non-reactive and heavy enough to keep the fermenting food below the brine's surface.

Lids are another essential component. While some traditional methods simply cover the fermentation vessel with a cloth, modern fermentation often uses specialized lids. These can range from simple screw-on lids with airlocks that allow gases produced during fermentation to escape while preventing air from getting in, to more advanced lids designed to release pressure automatically.

A thermometer is an invaluable tool in fermentation, as temperature control is crucial for the success of the process. Different microorganisms thrive at different temperatures, and maintaining the right temperature range is essential for achieving the desired fermentation results. A kitchen thermometer or a stick-on thermometer for the outside of the fermentation vessel can be used to monitor the temperature.

pH meters or test strips are also necessary, especially for fermentations where the acidity level needs to be monitored for safety reasons. In vegetable fermentation, a pH of 4.6 or lower is generally required to ensure that harmful bacteria cannot survive.

For measuring ingredients, especially salt and water for brine, accurate scales and measuring jugs are necessary. Precision is essential in fermentation to maintain the correct salt balance, inhibiting unwanted bacteria while allowing fermentation to occur.

In addition to these primary tools, various other supplies can enhance the fermentation process. These include airlocks, which are devices used to let gases escape from the fermentation vessel while preventing air from entering. Fermentation airlocks are particularly useful for long-term fermentations, such as wine or beer making. Cleanliness and sanitation are paramount in fermentation to prevent contamination. This necessitates having supplies like non-reactive cleaning brushes for cleaning jars and vessels, and sanitizers that are safe for use with food-grade equipment. Ensuring all equipment is thoroughly cleaned and sterilized before use is crucial in avoiding unwanted microbial growth.

Finally, the role of ingredients in fermentation cannot be overlooked. While technically not equipment, high-quality, fresh ingredients are essential for successful fermentation. This includes fresh, organic vegetables and fruits, non-iodized salt (as iodine can inhibit fermentation), and, in some cases, starter cultures or yeasts for specific types of fermentation.

In conclusion, the right equipment and supplies are fundamental to the art and science of fermentation. Each element plays a crucial role in ensuring a successful fermentation process, from the choice of fermentation vessels to the use of weights, lids, and temperature control tools. Additionally, maintaining cleanliness and using quality ingredients are just as important. With these tools and supplies, one can explore the vast and diverse world of fermentation, creating an array of flavors and textures in foods that are not only delicious but also nutritious. Whether a beginner or an experienced fermenter, understanding and assembling the proper equipment is the first step in transforming ordinary ingredients into extraordinary fermented foods.

Choosing the Right Vegetables and Ingredients

Choosing the right vegetables and ingredients for culinary endeavors is a fundamental step that significantly impacts a dish's flavor, texture, and overall success. This principle is particularly pertinent in cooking, pickling, and fermentation, where the intrinsic qualities of the ingredients play a pivotal role. In this section, we will explore the nuances of selecting the right vegetables and ingredients, focusing on aspects such as freshness, seasonality, variety, and their specific uses in culinary practices.

The cornerstone of any good cooking is the use of fresh ingredients. Freshness in vegetables is not just about their recent harvest but also their vibrancy, texture, and flavor. Fresh vegetables usually have a bright, natural color and a firm texture and are free from blemishes and rot. These attributes are crucial as they directly influence the taste and appearance of the final dish. In cooking, fresh vegetables provide the crisp textures and vivid flavors that are often the highlights of a meal. Freshness is even more critical in pickling and fermentation, as the quality of the vegetables can affect the safety and success of the preservation process.

Seasonality plays a significant role in the selection of vegetables. Seasonal produce is likely to be fresher, more flavorful, and nutritionally superior since it is harvested at the peak of its growth. Using seasonal vegetables also supports sustainable practices by reducing the carbon footprint associated with transportation of out-of-season produce. Each season brings its bounty; for instance, summer offers many choices like tomatoes, cucumbers, and bell peppers, while winter provides hardy vegetables like cabbages and root vegetables. Understanding and utilizing seasonal produce can elevate the quality of both cooked and preserved foods.

The variety of vegetables chosen is another critical consideration. Different varieties of the same vegetable can have distinct flavors, textures, and cooking or preserving qualities. For example, in the world of tomatoes, a beefsteak variety might be excellent for sandwiches and salads due to its size and juiciness, whereas Roma tomatoes are better suited for sauces and canning due to their lower moisture content and firmer texture. In pickling and fermentation, the choice of vegetable variety can affect the fermentation rate and the final product's flavor. For example, pickling cucumbers are preferred over regular ones for their firmer texture and smaller seeds, making them more suitable for the pickling process.

Beyond the choice of vegetables, the selection of other ingredients, such as herbs, spices, oils, and acids, plays a significant role in the culinary process. Herbs and spices can transform a simple dish into an aromatic and flavorful experience. The key is to choose herbs and spices that complement and enhance the natural flavors of the vegetables. Fresh herbs usually provide a brighter flavor in cooking, while dried herbs offer a more concentrated and earthy tone. The choice of oil can also influence a dish's flavor and nutritional content. Olive oil, for instance, is known for its heart-healthy properties and is favored in Mediterranean cooking, while sesame oil is often used in Asian cuisine for its distinct flavor.

In the realm of pickling and fermentation, the use of salt, vinegar, and sugar is critical. Non-iodized salt is a staple in these processes as iodine can interfere with fermentation. The type of vinegar used can vary based on the desired flavor profile; apple cider vinegar, for instance, imparts a fruitier taste than white vinegar. Sugar, when used, can balance the acidity and add a subtle sweetness.

In conclusion, carefully selecting vegetables and ingredients is fundamental to successful culinary practices. Freshness, seasonality, variety, and the complementary use of herbs, spices, and other ingredients are key considerations that can significantly enhance the quality of cooked, pickled, or fermented foods. By paying attention to these details, one can ensure that the foods' flavors, textures, and nutritional values are optimized, leading to more enjoyable and satisfying culinary experiences. Whether one is cooking a simple meal, pickling vegetables for winter, or experimenting with fermentation, the thoughtful choice of ingredients forms the foundation of great food.

Troubleshooting Common Fermentation Problems

While an ancient and generally straightforward culinary process, fermentation can occasionally present challenges even to the most experienced practitioners. Troubleshooting these issues requires understanding the fermentation process and the factors that can affect it. This section explores common problems encountered during fermentation, their causes, and potential solutions to ensure a successful ferment.

One of the most frequent issues in fermentation is the development of mold or unwanted bacteria. This usually appears as a white, green, or black fuzzy growth on the surface of the ferment. The primary cause of mold is exposure to air or contamination from improperly cleaned equipment. To prevent this, ensuring that all equipment is thoroughly sterilized before use and that the vegetables or fruits are completely submerged in the brine is crucial. If mold does appear, removing the affected area and continuing the fermentation is often safe, provided the mold has not penetrated deeply into the ferment.

Another common challenge is the failure of the fermentation to start, which can be indicated by a lack of bubbles or the expected change in taste or aroma. This problem can arise from several factors, such as insufficient salt, incorrect temperature, or the use of chlorinated water which can inhibit the growth of beneficial bacteria. Ensuring the correct salt concentration and using filtered or dechlorinated water can help, as can maintaining the ferment at an appropriate temperature for the specific bacteria or yeast involved.

Sometimes, a ferment may develop an off-flavor, becoming overly sour, bitter, or putrid. Several factors, including over-fermentation, contamination, or an imbalance in the microbial community can cause this issue. It's essential to taste the ferment regularly and to refrigerate it once it reaches the desired flavor profile to slow down further fermentation. If contamination is suspected, it's often best to discard the batch to avoid potential health risks.

Kahm yeast is another common issue, identified by a thin, white, filmy layer that forms on the surface of the ferment. While not harmful, it can impart an unpleasant flavor and should be removed. This yeast often develops in conditions with too much oxygen or the ferment is too alkaline. Ensuring a proper seal on the fermentation vessel and the correct salt concentration can prevent its occurrence.

Vegetables becoming soft or mushy is a frequent complaint, especially in long-term ferments. This can be caused by enzymatic activity or over-fermentation. To prevent this, some fermenters add tannin-rich ingredients like grape leaves or oak leaves, which can help maintain crispness. Additionally, monitoring the fermentation process and refrigerating the ferment once it reaches the desired texture can prevent over-fermentation.

A lack of acidity or tang in the final product can also occur, particularly in lactic acid fermentations like sauerkraut or kimchi. This issue may arise from insufficient fermentation time or a salt concentration that is too high, which can inhibit bacterial activity. Allowing more time for fermentation or adjusting the salt ratio can remedy this.

In alcoholic fermentation, such as in homebrewing beer or wine, a common problem is a stuck fermentation, where the yeast stops converting sugar into alcohol before it has consumed all available sugars. This can be due to various factors including insufficient nutrients for the yeast, incorrect temperature, or a high concentration of alcohol that inhibits yeast activity. Adjusting the temperature, aerating the ferment, or adding yeast nutrients can help restart a stuck fermentation.

Lastly, cross-contamination between different types of ferments can lead to unexpected results. This is particularly true in environments where multiple fermentation processes are co-occurring. To avoid this, it's important to separate different ferments and to practice good hygiene, including washing hands and sterilizing equipment between handling different ferments.

In conclusion, while fermentation is generally a robust and forgiving process, it can present challenges that require careful attention and troubleshooting. Common issues like mold, kahm yeast, off-flavors, and textural changes can often be prevented or remedied through proper technique, cleanliness, and environmental control. By understanding these potential problems and their solutions, enthusiasts can ensure the success and safety of their fermentation projects, resulting in delicious and nutritious fermented foods and beverages.

CHAPTER III

Recipes for Pickling

Dill Pickles

Dill pickles, a staple in many cuisines, are more than just a condiment or a crunchy snack; they are a culinary tradition steeped in history, flavor, and the art of preservation. This section explores the world of dill pickles, from their origins to the pickling process, their cultural significance, and the variations within this seemingly simple food item.

The history of dill pickles dates back to ancient times, with records indicating that pickling as a preservation method was used over 4000 years ago. While it is unclear when dill was first added to pickles, this herb has long been used in European and Asian cuisines for its flavor and preservative properties. The dill pickle as we know it today likely originated in Eastern Europe, where pickling was a standard method for preserving cucumbers, mainly for consumption during long winters when fresh vegetables were scarce.

The basic ingredients of a dill pickle are simple: cucumbers, water, vinegar, salt, and dill. Garlic, spices like mustard seeds, peppercorns, and sometimes sugar are also commonly added for extra flavor. The cucumbers are cleaned and often cut into spears or slices, although they can also be pickled whole. The fresh or dried dill imparts a distinctive tangy and slightly sweet flavor that is characteristic of dill pickles.

The process of making dill pickles can vary, but it typically involves either fermenting the cucumbers in a brine solution or immersing them in vinegar. In the traditional fermentation method, cucumbers are placed in a jar with dill, garlic, spices, and a saltwater brine. This jar is then left at room temperature for several days to several weeks, depending on the desired level of sourness. During this time, natural bacteria ferment the sugars in the cucumbers, producing lactic acid which acts as a natural preservative. The result is a tangy, crunchy pickle with probiotic properties.

The quicker vinegar method, also known as quick pickling, involves boiling a mixture of water, vinegar, salt, and spices, and pouring this hot liquid over the cucumbers and dill in jars. These jars are then sealed and left to cool, infusing the cucumbers with the brine flavors. This method is faster than traditional fermentation, producing more pronounced vinegar flavor pickles.

Dill pickles are not just a tasty snack; they are also nutritious. Cucumbers are low in calories but high in water content and contain several vitamins and minerals. The fermentation process can increase the bioavailability of these nutrients and introduce beneficial bacteria, making fermented dill pickles a probiotic food. Moreover, the spices and herbs used in pickling, such as dill and garlic, have their own health benefits, including anti-inflammatory and antioxidant properties.

Culturally, dill pickles have significance in many parts of the world. In the United States, they are a popular side dish, often served with sandwiches or hamburgers. In Eastern Europe, pickles are a traditional accompaniment to many dishes and are a staple at holiday feasts. They are also essential in many Jewish cuisines, particularly kosher-style delis.

There are numerous variations of dill pickles across different cuisines. Some variations include using different types of vinegar, such as apple cider or white vinegar, or adding unique spices and flavors. For example, in some cultures, a small amount of sugar is added to the brine for a sweeter pickle. The texture of dill pickles can also vary, from very crunchy to slightly soft, depending on the pickling process and the type of cucumber used.

In conclusion, dill pickles are a remarkable fusion of simplicity and complexity. They represent a method of preservation that has stood the test of time, extending the shelf life of cucumbers and transforming them into a flavorful, nutritious food. From their humble beginnings to their modern-day variations, dill pickles are a beloved food item, enjoyed for both their taste and health benefits. Whether served as a side, a snack, or a condiment, dill pickles are a testament to the enduring appeal of pickled foods in cuisines worldwide.

Bread and Butter Pickles

Bread and butter pickles, a classic American condiment, hold a unique place in the culinary world with their distinctive sweet and tangy flavor. This section delves into the history, preparation, and cultural significance of bread and butter pickles, shedding light on their enduring popularity and varied uses in cuisine.

The origin of bread and butter pickles is rooted in the United States during the Great Depression. The name "bread and butter" was coined during this period, supposedly because these pickles were a cheap and flavorful addition to meals, particularly as a complement to bread and butter during hard economic times. The exact origin story varies, but it is widely agreed that these pickles were a staple in many American households due to their ease of preparation and the ability to preserve excess cucumber harvests.

Bread and butter pickles are made from thinly sliced cucumbers, typically of the smaller, pickling variety. The cucumbers are mixed with sliced onions and salted to draw out excess water, which helps to keep them crisp. After rinsing and draining, the cucumbers and onions are covered with a pickling solution typically made of vinegar, sugar, and a blend of spices like mustard seed, celery seed, and turmeric. The sweetness of the sugar combined with the tanginess of the vinegar and the aroma of the spices creates a uniquely balanced flavor profile.

The preparation of bread and butter pickles falls under the category of quick pickling. Unlike fermented pickles, which can take weeks to mature, bread and butter pickles are ready to eat within a few hours or days of preparation. This quick pickling process involves heating the vinegar solution and pouring it over the cucumbers and onions, then sealing them in jars. The heat from the solution slightly cooks the cucumbers, allowing them to absorb the flavors more readily. The pickles are then left to cool and typically refrigerated, where they continue to develop their flavor.

Regarding nutritional value, bread and butter pickles offer a mix of benefits and considerations. Cucumbers themselves are low in calories and contain essential nutrients like vitamin K. However, the high sugar and sodium content in bread and butter pickles means that they should be consumed in moderation, especially for those monitoring their sugar and salt intake.

Culturally, bread and butter pickles have become a beloved part of American cuisine. They are commonly served as a side dish or as a topping on sandwiches and burgers, adding a sweet and tangy crunch that complements various flavors. Their versatility makes them a popular choice in home kitchens and restaurants alike. Furthermore, bread and butter pickles are often a gateway for home cooks to explore the world of pickling, as their simple preparation process and delicious results encourage beginners.

The popularity of bread and butter pickles has led to various adaptations and innovations. Some recipes add other vegetables like bell peppers or carrots for additional flavor and color. Others experiment with the spice mix, adding ingredients like hot peppers for a spicy kick or varying the sugar-to-vinegar ratio for a sweeter or tangier pickle.

In conclusion, bread and butter pickles are more than just a condiment; they are a testament to the ingenuity of home cooking, especially during challenging times. Their perfect balance of sweet, tangy, and spicy flavors has won the hearts of many and cemented their place in the American culinary landscape. The simplicity of their preparation makes them an excellent project for those new to pickling, while their versatility in recipes allows for endless culinary creativity. Whether enjoyed on their own or as part of a larger dish, bread and butter pickles continue to be a delightful and cherished part of American cuisine.

Pickled Peppers

Pickled peppers, a vibrant and flavorful addition to many cuisines, are a testament to the transformative power of pickling. This section explores the world of pickled peppers, from their historical origins to their preparation, varieties, and culinary uses, highlighting how this simple preservation technique has yielded a versatile and beloved ingredient.

The practice of pickling peppers likely began as a necessity, a way to preserve the harvest of peppers for use throughout the year. The exact origins are hard to pinpoint, as many cultures worldwide have a long history of pickling various foods, including peppers. However, it is clear that pickled peppers have been a part of human diets for centuries, if not millennia. The process extended the peppers' shelf life and enhanced their flavors, adding a new dimension to dishes.

Pickling peppers is a relatively straightforward process that can be varied in many ways to produce different flavors and textures. The primary method involves submerging the peppers in vinegar, water, and salt brine. Additional flavors are often added through spices like garlic, dill, mustard seeds, and bay leaves. The acidity of the vinegar acts as a preservative, allowing the peppers to be stored for extended periods. In some cases, sugar is added to the brine for a balance of sweetness, or the peppers are first fermented to develop their sourness before being pickled in vinegar.

A wide variety of peppers can be pickled, ranging from mild bell peppers to fiery hot chilis. Each type of pepper brings its unique level of heat, sweetness, and flavor to the pickling process. Bell peppers, for instance, become sweet and tangy when pickled, making them a great addition to salads and sandwiches. Hotter varieties, like jalapeños or habaneros, retain much of their heat and are ideal for adding a spicy kick to a dish.

The texture of pickled peppers is another crucial aspect. The time the peppers are left in the brine can affect their crunchiness. Shorter pickling times result in a firmer texture, while longer periods can make them softer. Additionally, the method of cutting the peppers - whether sliced, diced, or left whole - can also influence the texture and how the peppers absorb the pickling flavors.

Nutritionally, pickled peppers offer several benefits. Peppers are rich in vitamins A and C; pickling can help preserve these nutrients. However, it's worth noting that pickled peppers can be high in sodium due to the salt used in brining, so they should be consumed in moderation.

In terms of culinary use, pickled peppers are incredibly versatile. They can be used as a condiment, adding a burst of flavor and color to dishes like tacos, pizzas, sandwiches, and salads. They are also a common ingredient in antipasto platters and are often served alongside cheeses and cured meats. In cooking, pickled peppers can be used to add depth and brightness to sauces, stews, and marinades.

The cultural significance of pickled peppers varies around the world. In the Mediterranean, pickled peppers are a staple in many traditional dishes. In Mexico and the southwestern United States, pickled jalapeños are essential in local cuisines. Similarly, in Eastern European countries, pickled peppers are often used to flavor hearty winter meals.

In conclusion, pickled peppers are a remarkable example of how a simple preservation method can result in a product that is not only practical but also delicious and versatile. They are a staple ingredient in many cuisines worldwide, valued for their ability to enhance a wide variety of dishes. Whether providing a spicy kick, a sweet tang, or a vibrant burst of color, pickled peppers are a beloved addition to many kitchens. Their popularity is a testament to the enduring appeal of pickled foods and the endless culinary possibilities they offer.

Pickled Beets

Pickled beets are a vibrant and flavorful delicacy that have graced tables for generations, offering a unique combination of sweet, tangy, and earthy flavors. This section delves into the world of pickled beets, exploring their historical roots, culinary preparation, nutritional benefits, and the role they play in various cuisines across the globe.

The tradition of pickling beets has deep historical roots, likely originating in Eastern Europe, a region renowned for its extensive pickling culture. The practice began as a necessity to preserve the bountiful beet harvest for consumption during the long winter months. Over time, pickled beets transcended their humble beginnings as a preservation method, evolving into a beloved culinary item savored for their unique taste and vibrant color.

The process of pickling beets typically involves cooking the beets until tender, then slicing or cubing them before submerging in a pickling solution. This solution usually consists of vinegar, water, sugar, and salt, along with spices such as cloves, cinnamon, and mustard seeds, which impart additional flavors. The natural sweetness of beets balances beautifully with the acidity of the vinegar, while the spices add a complex flavor profile. The result is a versatile condiment that can add a pop of color and a burst of flavor to any meal.

One of the most striking aspects of pickled beets is their deep, rich color, which comes from betalains, natural pigments present in beets. This vibrant hue not only makes pickled beets visually appealing but also indicates the presence of powerful antioxidants. Beets are also rich in nutrients, including fiber, folate, and vitamin C. While adding some sodium and sugar, the pickling process largely preserves these beneficial nutrients, making pickled beets a healthy addition to diets.

In terms of culinary applications, pickled beets are extraordinarily versatile. They can be enjoyed on their own as a snack or used to enhance salads, sandwiches, and appetizers with their unique flavor and color. In Scandinavian countries, pickled beets are often paired with dishes like herring or served alongside potatoes and meats. In Eastern European cuisine, they are a common component of salads and cold plates. Pickled beets can also be pureed into dips and sauces, offering traditional recipes a sweet and tangy twist.

The nutritional aspect of pickled beets is also noteworthy. Beets are known for their health benefits, including improving blood flow and lowering blood pressure. While pickling adds vinegar and salt, it also preserves many vital nutrients in beets. For those conscious of sodium intake, it's important to moderate consumption of pickled beets or opt for versions with lower salt content.

Culturally, pickled beets hold a place in various food traditions. In North America, they are often found on holiday tables and are a staple in many home gardens and pantries. In European countries, especially in the East, pickled beets are part of the culinary heritage, often accompanying traditional dishes. Their versatility and ease of preparation have made them a beloved ingredient in many cultures, embraced for both their flavor and health benefits.

The popularity of pickled beets has grown globally, with chefs and home cooks alike experimenting with different pickling spices and techniques to create unique variations. Some contemporary recipes play with additional ingredients like onions, oranges, or ginger, adding new dimensions to the traditional flavor profile. This adaptability speaks to pickled beets' enduring appeal and ability to meld with various culinary styles.

In conclusion, pickled beets are a delightful and nutritious component of many cuisines, offering a unique blend of sweet, tangy, and earthy flavors. Their bright color, rich in antioxidants, adds visual appeal to dishes, while their versatility makes them a favored ingredient in various culinary preparations. From their roots in Eastern European preservation methods to their place in modern kitchens worldwide, pickled beets continue to be celebrated for their taste, nutritional value, and the vibrancy they bring to the culinary landscape. Whether served as a simple side dish, incorporated into salads, or used as a creative component in gourmet cooking, pickled beets remain a timeless and cherished food tradition.

Pickled Asparagus

Pickled asparagus, a culinary delicacy, combines the tender, earthy flavors of fresh asparagus with the tangy zest of pickling, creating a unique and sophisticated treat. This section explores the art and appeal of pickled asparagus, examining its historical roots, preparation methods, nutritional value, and its versatile role in modern gastronomy.

The history of pickling asparagus stretches back centuries, likely originating in regions where asparagus was native and abundant. Pickling, an ancient method of food preservation, provided a way to extend the shelf life of seasonal produce like asparagus beyond its short natural growing season. While the practice of pickling asparagus is not as widely documented as other pickled vegetables, it has been a part of European culinary traditions, especially in Mediterranean regions where asparagus grows prolifically.

The process of pickling asparagus begins with the selection of fresh, tender stalks. Young, firm asparagus spears are ideal for pickling, maintaining their texture and absorbing flavors well. The asparagus is typically washed and then blanched briefly to retain its vibrant green color and crisp texture. The pickling solution usually consists of vinegar, water, and salt, and often includes a variety of spices such as garlic, dill, mustard seeds, and peppercorns. Sugar may also be added to balance the acidity of the vinegar.

Once prepared, the asparagus and spices are packed into jars, and the hot pickling liquid is poured over them. The jars are then sealed and left to cool, allowing the flavors to meld and infuse the asparagus. This pickling process preserves the asparagus and transforms its flavor profile, adding a delectable tanginess that complements its natural earthiness.

Nutritionally, pickled asparagus offers several benefits. Asparagus is a nutrient-dense vegetable, rich in vitamins A, C, and K, as well as folate and fiber. It also contains antioxidants, including glutathione, known for its detoxifying properties. The pickling process can reduce some of these nutrients, particularly water-soluble vitamins, but many of the benefits remain intact. However, like most pickled foods, pickled asparagus can be high in sodium, so consumption should be moderated, especially for those on sodium-restricted diets.

In culinary applications, pickled asparagus is incredibly versatile. It can be enjoyed on its own as a snack or appetizer or used to add a unique flavor and texture to salads, charcuterie boards, and sandwiches. It is particularly popular as a garnish for cocktails, especially Bloody Marys, where its crispness and tangy flavor make it a perfect complement to the savory and spicy notes of the drink.

The cultural significance of pickled asparagus varies by region, but it has seen a surge in popularity in recent years, particularly in gourmet and artisanal food circles. This renewed interest is partly due to the growing trend of home pickling and fermentation, as well as an increased appreciation for seasonal and preserved foods.

Contemporary chefs and home cooks alike have experimented with pickling asparagus, creating various flavor combinations by using different types of vinegar, such as white wine or apple cider vinegar, and adding unique spices and herbs. This experimentation has led to various pickled asparagus products, from mildly tangy to boldly spiced, catering to diverse palates and culinary applications.

In conclusion, pickled asparagus is a delightful fusion of the delicate flavors of fresh asparagus and the bold, tangy notes of pickling. It exemplifies the art of transforming a simple vegetable into a gourmet ingredient through the time-honored method of pickling. Whether served as a sophisticated appetizer, a vibrant addition to a salad, or a unique garnish for a cocktail, pickled asparagus adds a touch of elegance and flavor to any culinary creation. Its nutritional benefits, coupled with its distinctive taste and versatility, make pickled asparagus a cherished item in kitchens around the world. As the interest in pickling and preserving foods continues to grow, pickled asparagus stands out as a testament to the enduring appeal of this ancient culinary practice.

Pickled Green Beans

Pickled green beans, a delightful fusion of crisp texture and tangy flavor, have emerged as a popular pickled delicacy in various culinary traditions. This section explores the intricate world of pickled green beans, delving into their history, preparation methods, nutritional value, and their culinary versatility and appeal.

Like many other vegetables, the practice of pickling green beans finds its roots in the ancient art of food preservation. Historical evidence suggests that pickling as a method to preserve food dates back over 4,000 years. While it is difficult to pinpoint the exact origin of pickled green beans, their existence is well-documented in various cuisines, particularly in Eastern European and American Southern cooking. The pickling process was essential before refrigeration, allowing surplus vegetables to be preserved and enjoyed throughout the year.

Creating pickled green beans begins with selecting fresh, crisp beans. The ideal candidates are young, tender beans that snap when bent, a sign of freshness and suitable texture. Preparation typically involves cleaning the beans and trimming their ends, followed by blanching—a quick immersion in boiling water followed by an ice bath—to retain their vibrant green color and crispness.

The brine, a critical component of pickling, is a mixture of vinegar, water, and salt. Variations in brine recipes are common, with some incorporating sugar for a sweet-and-sour effect, or spices such as garlic, dill, mustard seeds, and red pepper flakes to add depth and complexity to the flavor profile. The acidity of the vinegar not only imparts the characteristic tangy taste but also acts as a preservative, inhibiting the growth of spoilage-causing microorganisms.

Once prepared, the green beans are packed tightly into jars along with the chosen spices, and the hot brine is poured over them. The jars are then sealed and left to cool, allowing the flavors to meld. This process, known as quick pickling, results in a product that is ready to consume within a few days and can be stored for several months.

Nutritionally, pickled green beans offer several benefits. Green beans are low in calories and rich in essential nutrients, including vitamins C and K, fiber, and folate. While pickling may reduce some of these nutrients, particularly vitamin C, it does not diminish their dietary fiber content. However, like other pickled products, pickled green beans are high in sodium, which should be considered when consuming them, particularly for those monitoring their salt intake.

In terms of culinary applications, pickled green beans are remarkably versatile. They can be enjoyed as a standalone snack, offering a healthier alternative to traditional snack foods. They are commonly used as a garnish in cocktails, particularly in Bloody Marys, where their crisp texture and tangy flavor complement the savory and spicy elements of the drink. Additionally, they are a flavorful addition to salads, charcuterie boards, and antipasto platters, and can be used as an ingredient in various dishes, adding a unique twist to traditional recipes.

The cultural significance of pickled green beans varies across different regions. In the Southern United States, they are a staple in home canning and are often served at gatherings and special occasions. In Eastern European countries, pickled green beans are a common component of traditional meals, reflecting the region's rich pickling heritage.

Contemporary culinary trends have seen an increased interest in home pickling and fermentation, with pickled green beans gaining popularity among home cooks and chefs alike. This resurgence is partly driven by a growing appreciation for artisanal and homemade foods, as well as a desire for healthier snack options.

In conclusion, pickled green beans are a delightful combination of texture, taste, and nutrition. They represent a creative and delicious way to preserve and enjoy one of nature's simplest vegetables. Whether served as a crunchy snack, a cocktail garnish, or a vibrant addition to a meal, pickled green beans bring a burst of flavor and a touch of culinary tradition to the table. Their ease of preparation and versatility in various dishes make them a beloved choice in kitchens worldwide, continuing the age-old practice of pickling for future generations to savor and enjoy.

Pickled Eggs

Pickled eggs, a staple in many cultures, are a unique combination of simplicity and intricate flavor. This section delves into the history, preparation, nutritional aspects, and culinary uses of pickled eggs, exploring how this traditional food item has maintained its popularity over the years.

The origins of pickled eggs can be traced back centuries, with their history deeply rooted in the need for preservation before the advent of modern refrigeration. While the exact beginnings of pickled eggs are unclear, they have been a part of English cuisine since at least the 19th century and have also been popular in various European and North American cultures. Traditionally, pickled eggs were made by farmers and those who kept chickens as a means to preserve excess eggs that were not immediately consumed.

The basic process of making pickled eggs begins with hard boiling the eggs and then peeling them once they are cooled. The peeled eggs are then submerged in a mixture of vinegar, water, salt, and often various spices. Common spices and flavorings include garlic, dill, bay leaves, cloves, mustard seeds, and beet juice for coloring. The eggs are then sealed in a jar with the pickling solution and left to marinate for several days to several weeks. During this time, the brine flavors infuse into the eggs, giving them a distinctive tangy taste and a firm yet tender texture.

One of the most intriguing aspects of pickled eggs is the variety of flavors that can be achieved. The choice of vinegar, ranging from apple cider to white or malt vinegar, significantly impacts the flavor profile. The addition of beet juice creates a strikingly colorful pickled egg, with the white of the egg taking on a deep reddish-purple hue, adding visual appeal to their already interesting taste. Some variations even include hot peppers or curry spices, catering to those who prefer a spicy kick.

Nutritionally, pickled eggs retain many of the benefits of regular eggs, being a good source of protein, vitamins, and minerals such as Vitamin B12, selenium, and choline. However, the pickling process does add a considerable amount of sodium, and the eggs should be consumed in moderation, especially by individuals who need to manage their salt intake.

In terms of culinary uses, pickled eggs are incredibly versatile. They are commonly found in pubs and bars, particularly in the UK, as a savory snack to accompany alcoholic beverages. In home cooking, they can be used similarly to hard-boiled eggs, such as in salads, as a protein-rich addition to meals, or simply as a flavorful snack. Their unique taste and texture also make them a conversation-starting appetizer at gatherings.

Culturally, pickled eggs hold a special place in various food traditions. In the United States, particularly in the Midwest and Pennsylvania Dutch country, they are a common sight at local markets and fairs. In the UK, they are a nostalgic pub food, often homemade and stored behind the bar. This cultural significance has helped maintain the popularity of pickled eggs, despite the advent of modern refrigeration methods.

Contemporary interest in fermentation and pickling as methods of food preservation and flavor enhancement has led to a resurgence in the popularity of pickled eggs. This renewed interest is part of a broader trend towards traditional and artisanal food practices, where the simplicity and hands-on approach of pickling are valued.

In conclusion, pickled eggs are a fascinating example of a traditional food preservation method that has evolved into a beloved culinary item. Their rich history, the simplicity of preparation, and the depth of flavors they offer make pickled eggs a unique and enduring part of various culinary traditions. Whether enjoyed as a pub snack, a part of a meal, or a simple, protein-rich treat, pickled eggs continue to delight and satisfy with their distinctive tangy taste and firm texture. As the interest in pickling and traditional food practices grows, pickled eggs stand as a testament to the enduring appeal of this age-old preservation method.

Pickled Cucumbers

Pickled cucumbers, a global culinary phenomenon, stand as a testament to the versatility and enduring appeal of a simple vegetable transformed through the art of pickling. This section explores the history, preparation techniques, nutritional value, and culinary significance of pickled cucumbers, highlighting their role in diverse food cultures worldwide.

The history of pickling cucumbers dates back thousands of years, with evidence suggesting that the practice began in ancient Mesopotamia. The primary purpose of pickling was to preserve cucumbers beyond their growing season, ensuring a vegetable supply throughout the year. This preservation method spread across Europe, Asia, and eventually to the Americas, each culture adding its unique twist to the process and flavors.

The basic method of pickling cucumbers involves immersing them in a solution of vinegar, water, and salt. This mixture, often enhanced with spices such as dill, garlic, mustard seeds, and peppercorns, imparts a tangy flavor to the cucumbers. Sugar may also be added for a sweet-and-sour effect depending on the recipe. The pickling process varies from quick pickles, which are ready to eat within hours or days, to fermented pickles that develop over several weeks, offering a more complex flavor profile.

The variety of cucumbers chosen for pickling is critical to the quality of the final product. Smaller, firmer varieties, often called "pickling cucumbers," are preferred for their crisp texture and smaller seeds. These cucumbers are typically harvested before they reach full maturity, ensuring they remain crunchy after pickling.

Nutritionally, pickled cucumbers offer several health benefits, albeit with some considerations. Cucumbers are low in calories and contain essential nutrients such as vitamin K and potassium. The pickling process can also add probiotics to the cucumbers, particularly in fermented pickles, which are beneficial for gut health. However, pickled cucumbers can be high in sodium, and those with hypertension or needing to control sodium intake should consume them in moderation.

In the culinary world, pickled cucumbers are celebrated for their versatility. They are a staple in many cuisines, served as an accompaniment to meals, a flavorful addition to sandwiches and burgers, and a popular snack in their own right. In Eastern Europe, dill pickles are a key component of the traditional diet, often accompanying dishes like stews and sausages. In the United States, pickled cucumbers are synonymous with classic dill pickles, a favorite at barbecues and picnics. The tangy crunch of a pickled cucumber adds a welcome contrast to rich and savory dishes.

The cultural significance of pickled cucumbers varies globally, but their presence is ubiquitous. In Japanese cuisine, pickled cucumbers are part of tsukemono, a selection of pickled foods served with rice as a palate cleanser. In the Middle East, pickled cucumbers, often seasoned with mint and garlic, are a typical side dish. The adaptability of pickled cucumbers to different flavor profiles and cuisines is a key factor in their widespread popularity.

Modern culinary trends have seen a resurgence in pickling, with pickled cucumbers being a favorite subject of experimentation. Artisanal producers and home cooks alike are exploring new flavor combinations, using various vinegars, spices, and herbs to create unique and gourmet versions of this classic pickle.

In conclusion, pickled cucumbers are a remarkable representation of the simplicity and ingenuity of traditional food preservation techniques. Their crisp texture, tangy flavor, and nutritional benefits have made them a beloved ingredient in kitchens worldwide. From their historical origins as a necessity to their modern status as a versatile and sought-after food item, pickled cucumbers remain a staple in everyday and gourmet cuisine. Whether enjoyed as a snack, a side dish, or a flavorful addition to a meal, pickled cucumbers are a testament to this humble vegetable's enduring appeal and versatility.

CHAPTER IV

Recipes for Fermentation

Sauerkraut

Sauerkraut, a fermented cabbage dish, is a testament to the ingenuity of traditional food preservation methods. This section delves into the origins, preparation, health benefits, and cultural significance of sauerkraut, revealing how this humble dish has become a global culinary staple.

The history of sauerkraut extends back over 2,000 years, with roots that are often traced to China, where laborers building the Great Wall fermented cabbage in rice wine to preserve it. The concept eventually spread to Europe, particularly Germany, where the version we are familiar with today — fermented in its own juice — was developed. The name "sauerkraut," which translates to "sour cabbage" in German, reflects this evolution.

The process of making sauerkraut is a model of culinary simplicity yet biochemical complexity. It starts with finely shredded cabbage that is mixed with salt. The salt draws out water from the cabbage, creating a brine to ferment. The cabbage is then tightly packed into a jar or crock, submerged under its own liquid to create an anaerobic environment. Over the course of several weeks, naturally occurring lactic acid bacteria ferment the sugars in the cabbage, transforming it into sauerkraut. The result is a tangy, crunchy product that has a long shelf life and boasts enhanced flavors and nutritional benefits.

One of the most significant aspects of sauerkraut is its health benefits. Rich in vitamins C and K, fiber, and antioxidants, sauerkraut is a nutrient-dense food. Its real claim to fame, however, lies in its probiotic properties. The fermentation process encourages the growth of beneficial bacteria, which are known to aid digestion and promote a healthy gut microbiome. Regular consumption of sauerkraut can therefore contribute to improved digestive health, among other benefits.

Sauerkraut's culinary versatility is remarkable. It can be enjoyed straight from the jar, as a side dish, or used as an ingredient in various recipes. In German cuisine, sauerkraut is famously served with sausages, pork, and potatoes, creating a harmony of flavors. It's also a key ingredient in the Alsatian dish choucroute garnie and is popular in Eastern European cuisines, often accompanying pierogis or meats. In the United States, sauerkraut has become synonymous with Reuben sandwiches and as a topping for hot dogs.

The cultural significance of sauerkraut is profound. It is a staple food in Germany and Eastern Europe, integral to many traditional dishes and festivities. Its popularity in the United States, particularly among communities with German or Eastern European heritage, underscores its cultural importance. Sauerkraut is more than just food; it's a link to cultural identity and heritage.

The modern resurgence of interest in fermented foods has brought sauerkraut back into the culinary limelight. Health-conscious consumers and gourmet chefs alike are rediscovering sauerkraut, not only for its probiotic qualities but also for its unique taste and culinary potential. This has led to a new wave of artisanal sauerkraut producers experimenting with additional flavors — incorporating ingredients like caraway seeds, apples, or beets — thus expanding the traditional taste profile of this classic dish.

In terms of nutrition, sauerkraut is a low-calorie, high-fiber food that offers a range of health benefits. It is particularly rich in vitamin C, making it valuable during long winters when fresh fruits and vegetables were historically scarce. The fermentation process also produces compounds that may have anti-cancer properties and can improve digestive health.

Despite its numerous health benefits, sauerkraut should be consumed in moderation, especially by those with salt-sensitive hypertension, as it can be high in sodium. Furthermore, while fermentation enhances certain nutrients, it can also reduce others, such as B vitamins. In

conclusion, sauerkraut is a remarkable testament to the power of fermentation, a process that not only preserves food but also enhances its nutritional value and flavor. Its journey from ancient China to modern kitchens worldwide is a culinary migration and adaptation story. Sauerkraut's enduring popularity is a reflection of its versatility, health benefits, and unique taste, securing its place in the pantheon of celebrated fermented foods. As the world continues to embrace traditional methods of food preservation, sauerkraut stands as a symbol of cultural heritage and gastronomic innovation.

Kimchi

Kimchi, a staple in Korean cuisine, is much more than a side dish. It is a symbol of cultural heritage, a testament to the art of fermentation, and a culinary delight savored around the globe. This section explores the rich history, intricate preparation, nutritional benefits, and cultural significance of kimchi, a dish that transcends mere sustenance to become an emblem of a nation's culinary identity.

The origins of kimchi can be traced back to ancient Korea, where it began as a way to preserve vegetables for the winter months. Early forms of kimchi were simple, consisting mainly of fermented vegetables. With the introduction of New World crops like chili peppers in the

17th century, kimchi evolved into the spicy, flavorful dish known today. This transformation marked a significant turning point in the history of kimchi, embedding it deeply into Korean culture and cuisine.

The preparation of kimchi involves a meticulous and labor-intensive process, reflecting the Korean ethos of dedication and precision in culinary arts. Traditionally, kimchi is made by first salting the main vegetable, usually napa cabbage or Korean radish, to remove water and to create an environment conducive to fermentation. The next step involves mixing the vegetables with various seasonings, including chili pepper flakes, garlic, ginger, scallions, and a range of other ingredients like fish sauce or fermented shrimp paste. This mixture is then packed tightly in jars or earthenware pots called "onggi" and left to ferment at room temperature for a few days before being stored in cool temperatures.

The fermentation process, led primarily by lactic acid bacteria, not only preserves the vegetables but also enhances their flavors and nutritional value. The result is a tangy, spicy, and deeply flavorful dish, with a crunchy texture that is both appealing and satisfying.

Kimchi's nutritional profile is as impressive as its taste. It is low in calories but high in fiber, vitamins A and C, and beneficial probiotics that are crucial for gut health. Fermentation also amplifies certain nutrients, making kimchi a powerhouse of dietary benefits. Regular kimchi consumption has been linked to various health benefits, including improved digestion, boosted immunity, and even potential weight loss properties.

The cultural significance of kimchi in Korea cannot be overstated. It is a dish at almost every meal, reflecting the Korean belief in balance and harmony in food. Kimchi is not just food; it represents a connection to the land, a sense of community, and a link to the past. The art of making kimchi is often passed down through generations, with recipes varying from region to region and family to family, each with its unique blend of flavors and ingredients.

The popularity of kimchi has spread far beyond Korea's borders, gaining a place in the global culinary scene. It has been embraced by chefs and food enthusiasts worldwide, who admire its complex flavor profile and health benefits. This international recognition was highlighted when UNESCO designated Korea's kimchi-making tradition, known as "kimjang," as an intangible cultural heritage of humanity.

In recent years, kimchi has grown in popularity due to growing interest in fermented foods and their health benefits. It has become a staple in health food stores and is increasingly featured in fusion cuisine, demonstrating its versatility and adaptability to different culinary styles.

In conclusion, kimchi is more than just a fermented vegetable dish; it is an integral part of Korean culture and cuisine, a symbol of national pride, and a testament to the timeless art of fermentation. Its complex flavors, nutritional benefits, and cultural significance have earned it a revered place in the world of gastronomy. As global interest in fermentation and healthful eating continues to grow, kimchi stands out as a culinary treasure, offering a blend of history, flavor, and nutrition that is unmatched by any other dish. Whether enjoyed in its traditional form or as part of innovative culinary creations, kimchi continues to captivate palates and enrich diets worldwide.

Fermented salsa

Fermented salsa, a dynamic fusion of traditional salsa flavors with the ancient art of fermentation, presents a unique culinary experience. This section explores the concept, preparation, and benefits of fermented salsa, highlighting how this innovative adaptation of a classic condiment adds a depth of flavor and nutritional value to everyday meals.

Salsa, a ubiquitous condiment in Mexican and Tex-Mex cuisines, traditionally consists of tomatoes, onions, chili peppers, and various seasonings. While traditionally served fresh, the practice of fermenting salsa brings a new dimension to this staple. Fermentation, one of the oldest food preservation techniques, involves the conversion of carbohydrates to alcohol or organic acids using microorganisms—yeasts or bacteria—under anaerobic conditions. When applied to salsa, fermentation extends its shelf life and enhances its flavors and nutritional profile.

The process of making fermented salsa begins similarly to that of traditional salsa. Ingredients like ripe tomatoes, onions, garlic, chili peppers, and cilantro are finely chopped and mixed. The key difference lies in adding a saltwater brine, which creates an environment conducive to fermentation. Some recipes also include whey or a starter culture to kickstart the fermentation process, although many rely on the natural lactobacilli present on the vegetables. Once mixed, the salsa is placed in a jar, submerging the mixture under the brine to create an anaerobic environment. The jar is left at room temperature for several days, during which the fermentation process occurs.

During fermentation, lactobacilli convert sugars and starches present in the salsa ingredients into lactic acid. This preserves the salsa, gives it a distinctive tangy flavor, and develops a complex aroma. Fermentation also produces beneficial enzymes and probiotics, contributing to improved gut health.

One of the significant benefits of fermented salsa is its enhanced nutritional value. The lacto-fermentation process increases the availability of vitamins and minerals in the salsa, particularly vitamin C and B vitamins. The presence of probiotics, beneficial for gut flora, is another health advantage. These probiotics can aid in digestion, boost the immune system, and contribute to overall gut health.

Regarding culinary applications, fermented salsa can be used in much the same way as traditional salsa. It pairs excellently with tacos, burritos, and nachos, and can be used as a zesty topping for grilled meats or a flavorful dip for chips. However, it's important to note that cooking fermented salsa can destroy its probiotics, so it's best used in its raw form to reap the full health benefits.

Fermented salsa also holds cultural significance as it represents a blend of traditional food practices with contemporary culinary trends. While traditional salsa is a cornerstone of Mexican cuisine, the practice of fermenting foods is a global phenomenon, evident in various cultures worldwide. The fusion of these two traditions in fermented salsa is a reflection of the growing interest in combining culinary heritage with modern health consciousness.

The rising popularity of fermented foods has recently brought fermented salsa into the spotlight. As people become more aware of the health benefits of fermented foods, dishes like fermented salsa gain appeal among health enthusiasts and culinary experimenters who appreciate its unique flavor profile.

In conclusion, fermented salsa is an excellent example of how fermentation can adapt and revitalize traditional dishes. This process elevates the salsa flavors, making it tangier and more complex, and enhances its nutritional benefits, particularly in terms of probiotics and vitamin content. Fermented salsa straddles the line between a beloved traditional condiment and a healthful, probiotic-rich food, appealing to various palates and dietary preferences. As the trend towards healthier, gut-friendly foods continues, fermented salsa stands out as a delicious and nutritious choice, combining the best of both worlds – flavor and health.

Kombucha

Kombucha, a fermented tea beverage, has surged in popularity in recent years, becoming a staple in the diets of health-conscious consumers worldwide. This section explores kombucha's origins, brewing process, health benefits, and cultural impact, providing insight into why this ancient drink has become a modern-day phenomenon.

The history of kombucha is shrouded in mystery, with its origins believed to date back thousands of years. Some theories suggest that it originated in Northeast China around 220 B.C. and was initially prized for its healing properties. The tea was later introduced to Japan and Russia, gradually spreading across Europe and eventually to the rest of the world. Despite its ancient roots, kombucha remained relatively obscure until its recent resurgence in popularity, driven by an increasing interest in probiotic foods and natural health remedies.

Kombucha is created through a fermentation process that begins with a sweetened black or green tea base. The key to kombucha's fermentation is the symbiotic culture of bacteria and yeast (SCOBY), a gelatinous, living organism that transforms the sweet tea into kombucha. The SCOBY consumes the sugars in the tea, producing ethanol, carbon dioxide, and various acids, including acetic, gluconic, and glucuronic acids. This fermentation process, typically lasting between 7 to 30 days, results in a tangy, slightly effervescent beverage with a unique flavor that can vary from sweet to sour, depending on the duration of fermentation.

One of the most lauded aspects of kombucha is its purported health benefits. Kombucha is rich in probiotics, the beneficial bacteria that promote gut health. These probiotics can aid digestion, help restore balance in the gut microbiome, and improve overall gastrointestinal health. Kombucha also contains antioxidants, mainly when made with green tea, which can neutralize harmful free radicals in the body. Additionally, the tea is a source of B vitamins and may contain small amounts of alcohol and caffeine, depending on the brewing process.

However, it is essential to approach kombucha's health claims cautiously. While anecdotal evidence supports its health benefits, scientific research in this area is still emerging. Some studies suggest potential health benefits, but more comprehensive research is needed to substantiate these claims fully.

Regarding its cultural impact, kombucha has grown from a niche health food item to a mainstream beverage available in countless flavors and varieties. Its rise in popularity is partly due to the growing interest in fermented foods and beverages, which are sought after for their probiotic content and unique flavors. Kombucha has been embraced by health enthusiasts, fitness communities, and those seeking alternative, natural beverages.

The commercialization of kombucha has led to an explosion of brands and flavors, ranging from traditional recipes to innovative combinations incorporating herbs, spices, and fruit juices. This diversity has made kombucha appealing to a wide audience, with options catering to various taste preferences and dietary needs.

Brewing kombucha at home has also become popular, part of a broader trend towards DIY food projects and an interest in artisanal food production. Home brewing allows for customization of flavor and potency and can be a rewarding way to engage with the process of fermentation. The online community of kombucha enthusiasts shares recipes, techniques, and experiences, further fueling interest in this unique beverage.

In conclusion, kombucha represents the intersection of ancient tradition and modern health trends, a fermented beverage that has captured the attention of health-conscious consumers worldwide. Its complex flavor profile, potential health benefits, and cultural significance have made it a popular and intriguing beverage. Whether enjoyed for its taste, health properties, or as part of a lifestyle choice, kombucha has cemented its place in the landscape of contemporary health and wellness trends. As research continues to unravel the mysteries of fermentation and gut health, kombucha will likely remain a staple in the world of healthful beverages.

Yogurt

Yogurt, a creamy and tangy food, has been a staple in various cultures for thousands of years. Rich in history, nutrition, and culinary versatility, yogurt is not merely a food product but a representation of the confluence of biology, culture, and gastronomy. This section explores yogurt's origins, production process, health benefits, and cultural significance, offering insight into why this fermented dairy product is revered globally.

The history of yogurt is as old as human civilization, with its origins believed to date back to 5000 BC in Mesopotamia. While the exact genesis of yogurt is unknown, it is widely thought to have been discovered accidentally through the natural fermentation of milk in warm climates. The lactic acid bacteria present in milk fermented the lactose, transforming the milk into yogurt. This process preserved the milk and gave it a unique flavor and texture. Over centuries, yogurt spread across the Middle East, Central Asia, and into India and Eastern

Europe, becoming an integral part of many traditional diets.

The primary process of making yogurt involves fermenting milk with specific bacterial cultures, typically Lactobacillus bulgaricus and Streptococcus thermophilus. The process begins with heating the milk to denature the proteins, ensuring a smooth and thick end product. Once cooled to a warm temperature, the bacterial cultures are added. The mixture is then maintained at a steady temperature to allow the bacteria to ferment the lactose, the natural sugar in milk, producing lactic acid. This acid acts on milk protein to give yogurt its texture and tangy taste. The fermentation process can last anywhere from a few hours to overnight, depending on the desired thickness and sourness.

One of yogurt's most significant attributes is its health benefits. It is a rich source of essential nutrients, including calcium, protein, potassium, phosphorus, and vitamins B2 and B12. The fermentation process makes these nutrients more accessible and also produces probiotics, beneficial bacteria that support gut health. Regular yogurt consumption has been linked to various health benefits, including improved digestion, stronger immune function, and potential weight management benefits. Additionally, for individuals who are lactose intolerant, yogurt can often be more tolerable than milk due to the conversion of lactose into lactic acid by the bacterial cultures.

Yogurt's culinary uses are incredibly diverse, transcending cultural and geographical boundaries. It is consumed on its own or as a part of numerous dishes. In Indian cuisine, yogurt is a base for raitas, used as a marinade in dishes like tandoori chicken, and sweetened in desserts like lassi. In Middle Eastern countries, herbs and spices are often combined to make sauces such as tzatziki or eaten with meze. In Western cultures, yogurt is frequently consumed at breakfast, blended into smoothies, or served with fruit and granola. Its culinary versatility is evident in its ability to be incorporated into both sweet and savory dishes.

The cultural significance of yogurt is profound, with its production and consumption rooted in traditional practices. In many cultures, yogurt is not just a food but a symbol of hospitality and a staple in dietary customs. Making yogurt is a revered skill, often passed down through generations. In Bulgaria and Turkey, yogurt is a national symbol, deeply embedded in the country's culinary identity.

The modern global dairy market has seen a significant expansion in the various yogurts available. This includes a range of fat contents, from full-fat to fat-free, and the introduction of flavored yogurts, fruit yogurts, and yogurt-based drinks. The rise of plant-based diets has also led to the development of non-dairy yogurts made from almond, soy, and coconut milk.

Despite its widespread commercialization, the essence of traditional yogurt-making endures. Home yogurt-making remains popular, with many prefer homemade yogurt's taste and texture. This practice connects people to the simplicity and natural fermentation process, serving as a reminder of yogurt's humble origins.

In conclusion, yogurt is a testament to the simplicity and power of fermentation, a process that transforms milk into a food that is nutritious, delicious, and versatile. Its journey from ancient times to modern supermarket shelves is a culinary evolution and adaptation story. Whether consumed for its health benefits, as part of a cultural tradition, or simply for its taste, yogurt continues to be a beloved food across the globe. As we continue to explore the connections between diet, health, and culture, yogurt stands as a symbol of these intersections, a food that nourishes the body, delights the palate, and enriches our understanding of culinary history.

Fermented Hot Sauce

Fermented hot sauce, a fiery and flavorful condiment, is a fusion of the ancient art of fermentation with the culinary pursuit of spice and heat. This section delves into the intricacies of fermented hot sauce, covering its history, production process, health benefits, and its place in various culinary traditions, illuminating why this spicy concoction continues to tantalize taste buds worldwide.

The history of fermented hot sauce stretches back centuries, with roots intertwined with the history of chili peppers. Chili peppers, native to the Americas, were introduced to the rest of the world following Columbus's voyage in 1492. Fermentation, an ancient food preservation method, was likely applied to these peppers by various cultures independently, resulting in the birth of numerous regional hot sauces. These sauces extended the harvest's shelf life and enhanced the peppers' flavors and heat.

The primary ingredient in fermented hot sauce is chili peppers, ranging from milder varieties like jalapeños to fiery habaneros. The peppers are often combined with other ingredients such as garlic, onions, and various spices, to create layers of flavor. The fundamental element of the process is the fermentation of these ingredients, typically in a brine solution.

The fermentation process begins with submerging the peppers and other ingredients in a saltwater solution. This brine creates an anaerobic environment conducive to the growth of beneficial bacteria, particularly lactobacillus. As the bacteria consume the sugars in the peppers and other ingredients, they produce lactic acid, which acts as a natural preservative. The length of the fermentation can range from a few weeks to several months, with longer fermentations yielding more complex and developed flavors.

This process not only preserves the peppers but also transforms their flavors. The heat of the peppers melds with tangy, sometimes fruity, or smoky notes, resulting in a hot sauce that is rich and multifaceted. The level of heat in the final product can be controlled by the choice of peppers and the length of fermentation, allowing for a wide range of sauces from mildly spicy to intensely hot.

One of the significant benefits of fermented hot sauce is its health aspects. The fermentation process enhances the bioavailability of nutrients in the peppers, making them more beneficial. Capsaicin, the compound responsible for the heat in chili peppers, has been linked to various health benefits, including pain relief, reduced inflammation, and potential metabolism boosting properties. Probiotics in fermented hot sauces also contribute to improved gut health and digestion.

In terms of culinary applications, fermented hot sauce is incredibly versatile. It can be used to spice up various dishes, from tacos and pizzas to soups and marinades. The depth of flavor in fermented hot sauce also makes it an excellent ingredient in cooking, offering more than just heat – it can introduce a nuanced and complex flavor profile to dishes.

The cultural significance of fermented hot sauce varies around the globe. Hot sauce is a staple condiment in many regions, particularly in Latin America and the Caribbean, deeply ingrained in culinary traditions. Each region has its unique twist on hot sauce, with variations in ingredients and preparation methods reflecting local tastes and cultural influences.

The recent surge in the popularity of fermented foods has brought renewed attention to fermented hot sauces. This resurgence is part of a broader trend towards foods that are not only flavorful but also offer health benefits. Artisanal producers and home fermenters are experimenting with diverse ingredients and fermentation techniques, creating a wide array of hot sauces that cater to various palates.

In conclusion, fermented hot sauce is a vibrant embodiment of culinary tradition and innovation. It represents the melding of ancient preservation techniques with a modern appreciation for complex flavors and health benefits. The versatility of fermented hot sauce in cuisine, rich flavors, and healthful properties make it a cherished condiment for spice lovers and culinary adventurers alike. As interest in fermentation and spicy foods grows, fermented hot sauce stands out as a flavorful testament to the enduring appeal of heat and tang in our diets. Whether enjoyed as a fiery addition to a favorite dish or a key ingredient in a recipe, fermented hot sauce remains a beloved staple in kitchens worldwide.

Fermented Pickles

Fermented pickles, a delectable result of the ancient art of fermentation, are a culinary delight that combines the crispness of fresh cucumbers with tangy, complex flavors developed through natural processes. This section delves into fermented pickles' history, methods, nutritional benefits, and cultural significance, illuminating their role in various culinary traditions and their resurgence in contemporary gastronomy.

The history of fermented pickles is deeply rooted in the human need for preserving food. The practice dates back thousands of years, with evidence of pickling found in ancient Mesopotamia. Fermentation was a necessity before the advent of refrigeration, as it extended the shelf life of fresh produce like cucumbers. Various cultures worldwide have their distinct methods and traditions of pickle fermentation, but the fundamental principles remain consistent.

Making fermented pickles begins with fresh cucumbers, preferably smaller varieties known for their crisp texture. These cucumbers are submerged in a brine solution made of water and salt, sometimes with the addition of spices and herbs such as dill, garlic, mustard seeds, and peppercorns. Unlike vinegar-based pickles, fermented pickles rely on the natural lacto-fermentation process. Lactobacillus bacteria, naturally present on the skin of cucumbers, facilitate this process. When submerged in the brine, these bacteria convert sugars in the cucumbers into lactic acid, which acts as a natural preservative.

This fermentation process takes place over several days to weeks and is usually carried out at room temperature. During this time, the cucumbers undergo a remarkable transformation. The lactic acid produced not only preserves the cucumbers but also imparts a distinctive sour flavor characteristic of fermented pickles. This process also creates an environment that inhibits the growth of harmful bacteria, making fermented pickles a safe and healthy food choice.

One of the key benefits of fermented pickles is their nutritional value. They are a rich source of probiotics, the beneficial bacteria that play a crucial role in gut health. These probiotics can aid digestion, enhance nutrient absorption, and even contribute to a healthy immune system. Fermented pickles are also low in calories and a good source of vitamin K, essential for blood clotting and bone health. Moreover, the cucumbers themselves contain essential nutrients like vitamin C, potassium, and fiber.

Fermented pickles are more than just a side dish or condiment in culinary traditions. They are integral to many cuisines, celebrated for their unique flavors and textures. In Eastern Europe, fermented pickles are a staple, often served alongside hearty meals like stews and sausages. In the United States, they are synonymous with classic deli fare, adding a tangy crunch to sandwiches and burgers. In Korean cuisine, fermented pickles, or jangajji, are a common banchan (side dish), offering a refreshing counterpoint to spicy dishes.

The recent revival of interest in traditional fermentation methods has brought fermented pickles back into the culinary limelight. This resurgence is part of a broader trend towards natural, healthful eating practices. Fermented pickles are now celebrated for their taste and health benefits, particularly regarding gut health and natural food preservation.

Artisanal producers and home cooks are exploring the art of pickle fermentation with renewed enthusiasm, experimenting with various brine concentrations, fermentation times, and flavorings. This has led to a diverse array of fermented pickle products, each with its unique taste profile, ranging from mildly sour to intensely tangy.

In conclusion, fermented pickles represent a harmonious blend of culinary tradition, nutritional benefit, and gastronomic pleasure. They embody the simplicity and wisdom of ancient food preservation techniques while offering a healthful, probiotic-rich food choice. The versatility of fermented pickles in cuisine and their distinctive flavors and textures makes them a beloved ingredient in kitchens worldwide. As the interest in natural fermentation and health-conscious eating continues to grow, fermented pickles are a testament to the enduring appeal of traditionally preserved foods. Whether enjoyed as a snack, a side dish, or a key ingredient in a recipe, fermented pickles continue to captivate the palates of those who seek both flavor and nourishment in their culinary choices.

Fermented Garlic

Fermented garlic, a culinary ingredient rich in flavor and history, is a testament to the transformative power of fermentation. In this section, we explore the journey of garlic from a raw, pungent bulb to a mellow, umami-packed fermented delicacy. We examine its historical roots, fermentation process, nutritional benefits, and fermented garlic's role in various cuisines.

Garlic has been cultivated for thousands of years and is significant in many cultures for its culinary and medicinal properties. The practice of fermenting garlic is thought to have ancient origins, likely developed independently across different cultures as a method to preserve the garlic harvest. Fermented garlic, often known as black garlic, gained prominence in Asian cuisines, particularly in Korea, Thailand, and Japan, where it is valued for its unique flavor and health benefits.

The process of fermenting garlic involves a slow transformation under controlled conditions. Traditional methods include keeping the garlic at a steady temperature (usually between 60 to 90 degrees Celsius) and humidity for several weeks to months. During this time, the natural sugars and amino acids in garlic undergo the Maillard reaction, a chemical process that occurs between amino acids and reducing sugars in the presence of heat, developing a dark color, soft texture, and complex flavors.

Unlike other fermented products, fermented garlic does not involve the addition of salt or water. The process depends entirely on the garlic's natural moisture and sugar content. The resulting product, often called black garlic, is soft, chewy, with a molasses-like richness, and devoid of the raw garlic's sharp, pungent flavor. It acquires a sweet, umami taste, with hints of balsamic vinegar and tamarind.

Nutritionally, fermented garlic is a powerhouse. It retains the health benefits of raw garlic while developing additional properties through fermentation. Garlic is known for its high levels of antioxidants, compounds that protect against cellular damage. It also contains allicin, a potent medicinal compound with antibacterial and anti-inflammatory effects. The fermentation process is believed to increase the levels of certain antioxidants, making fermented garlic even more beneficial.

In culinary applications, fermented garlic is incredibly versatile. It can be used in place of regular garlic to add depth and complexity to dishes. Its milder, sweeter flavor makes it suitable for use in a broader range of dishes, including desserts. In Asian cuisine, fermented garlic is used in sauces, marinades, and as a condiment. It can also be spread on bread or crackers as a unique, flavorful spread.

The cultural significance of fermented garlic is notable, particularly in Asian countries where it is a staple in traditional medicine and cuisine. Its health benefits are highly regarded, with fermented garlic being consumed for its flavor and as a health supplement. It is believed to aid in digestion, boost immune function, and improve cardiovascular health.

The recent surge in popularity of fermented foods in the West has brought fermented garlic into the limelight. It is now celebrated not only for its unique taste but also for its health benefits. This has led to an increase in its availability in gourmet food stores and health food shops. The trend towards natural, health-promoting foods has further boosted its popularity.

In conclusion, fermented garlic is a shining example of the wonders of fermentation, a process that not only preserves food but also enhances its flavors and health benefits. It is a testament to the ingenuity of traditional culinary practices, adapting a common ingredient into something extraordinary. With its complex flavors and nutritional advantages, fermented garlic has found its place in the modern culinary world, bridging the gap between ancient traditions and contemporary health-conscious eating. Whether used in gourmet cooking or as a health supplement, fermented garlic continues to be a versatile and valued ingredient in kitchens and diets worldwide.

CHAPTER V

Combining Pickling and Fermentation

Creative Recipes Combining Both Techniques

The culinary world thrives on innovation and the fusion of techniques, and the combination of pickling and fermentation is a splendid example of this creativity. This section explores the intersection of these two methods, offering insight into how blending the sharp, tangy flavors of pickling with the complex, deep notes of fermentation can result in an array of intriguing and delightful recipes.

Though similar in their goal to preserve and enhance food, the art of pickling and fermentation operate on different principles. Pickling typically involves immersing foods in an acid solution, usually vinegar, along with various seasonings. Conversely, fermentation relies on natural bacteria to break down sugars and starches in food, producing lactic acid. When these two methods converge in a recipe, the outcome is a dish that marries the immediate zing of pickling with the layered, evolved flavors of fermentation.

One creative example of this fusion is a fermented pickle salsa. Traditional salsa ingredients like tomatoes, onions, cilantro, and chili peppers are first fermented to develop depth and umami flavors. The fermented mixture is then combined with a pickling solution of vinegar and sugar, adding a bright, sharp edge to the salsa. This recipe can be an excellent accompaniment to grilled meats or a vibrant dip for chips.

Another innovative recipe is the kimchi and pickled vegetable salad. In this dish, traditional Korean kimchi, made through fermentation, is tossed with various quick-pickled vegetables like carrots, cucumbers, and radishes. The result is a salad bursting with contrasting flavors – the deep, spicy, and tangy kimchi notes complementing the pickled vegetables' crisp, acidic bite.

Combining pickling and fermentation can also be explored in meat dishes. A concept could be fermented and pickled chicken. The chicken is first marinated in a fermented mixture of yogurt and spices, allowing it to tenderize and absorb complex flavors. After cooking, the chicken is finished with a pickling brine, adding a zesty and piquant flavor. This dish could represent a harmony of preservation techniques, offering a sensory journey through its layered flavors.

A fusion of pickling and fermentation techniques can also be seen in bread making. An example is sourdough rye bread with pickled seeds. This recipe uses traditional sourdough fermentation to create the bread, offering its characteristic tang and chewy texture. The dough can be embedded with seeds picked in vinegar and spices, providing bursts of sharp flavor in every bite.

Desserts, too, can benefit from this combination. Consider a fermented fruit compote with pickled zest. Seasonal fruits are fermented to enhance their sweetness and create a syrupy texture. This compote is then topped with finely shredded citrus zest that has been lightly pickled in a sweet vinegar solution, adding a bright, tangy note to the dessert.

In beverages, the fusion of pickling and fermentation can create unique cocktails and non-alcoholic drinks. A fermented berry and pickled ginger soda is one such example. Berries are fermented to develop a rich, deep flavor, then mixed with a syrup made from pickled ginger, which adds a spicy, tangy kick. When combined with sparkling water, this mixture creates a refreshing and complex drink.

These recipes are not just culinary experiments; they reflect a broader trend in the culinary world toward blending traditional methods for new, innovative flavors. The combination of pickling and fermentation allows chefs and home cooks to experiment with taste profiles, textures, and nutritional benefits, pushing the boundaries of conventional cuisine.

In conclusion, the creative combination of pickling and fermentation in recipes offers a culinary playground for exploration and innovation. This fusion enhances the flavors and textures of foods and merges the health benefits of both methods. As culinary arts continue to evolve, the intersection of different food preservation techniques like pickling and fermentation is a fertile ground for discovery, offering endless possibilities for new, exciting dishes. These recipes celebrate the heritage of traditional methods while embracing the creativity and diversity of modern cuisine, making them a delightful addition to any culinary repertoire.

Flavor Combinations and Innovations

The culinary landscape constantly evolves, with chefs and food enthusiasts continually pushing the boundaries of flavor and technique. In this realm, the art of pickling and fermentation stands out for its ability to transform ingredients and create complex, nuanced flavors. This section explores the myriad of flavor combinations and innovations achieved through pickling and fermentation, shedding light on how these age-old methods have been revitalized in contemporary gastronomy.

The essence of pickling and fermentation lies in their ability to preserve and enhance ingredients' natural flavors. While pickling often involves immersing foods in a solution of vinegar, salt, and various seasonings, fermentation relies on the action of natural bacteria, yeasts, or molds to convert organic substances into acids or alcohol. These processes extend the shelf life of foods and develop a depth of flavor that is difficult to replicate through other cooking methods.

Innovative flavor combinations in pickling and fermentation are vast and varied. One popular trend is the fusion of different cultural techniques and flavors. For instance, combining Korean kimchi fermentation methods with non-traditional ingredients like Brussels sprouts or apples can result in a unique blend of flavors – the traditional spicy and pungent notes of kimchi marrying beautifully with the sweetness and texture of these Western ingredients.

Another area of innovation is the use of pickling and fermentation in sweet applications. Fermented fruits, for example, can be used in desserts to add complexity and a slight tang. Imagine a vanilla panna cotta topped with lightly fermented berries – the creamy, sweet base is perfectly offset by the sharp, fruity notes of the berries, creating a harmonious balance on the palate.

Chefs are also exploring the use of pickled ingredients in cocktails and beverages. A cocktail with gin, tonic, and a splash of pickled beet juice offers an earthy depth and striking color, transforming a classic drink into a gourmet experience. Similarly, fermented ginger can be used to create a homemade ginger beer that is both zesty and rich in probiotics.

Traditionally overlooked vegetables in the pickling and fermentation process are now being rediscovered. With its bitter notes, pickled radicchio can add an intriguing flavor to salads and sandwiches. Spiced with cinnamon and star anise, fermented sweet potatoes can be a surprising and delightful side dish.

In the realm of proteins, pickling and fermentation are being used to tenderize and flavor meats and fish.

Fermented fish sauce, a staple in Southeast Asian cuisines, is being incorporated into marinades and dressings for its umami-rich profile. Pickled shrimp, a Southern delicacy, is gaining popularity for its ability to infuse the shellfish with bright, acidic flavors.

The health benefits of fermented and pickled foods are also driving innovation. Fermented foods are known for their probiotic qualities, beneficial for gut health. Chefs are integrating these foods into dishes not only for their flavor but also for their nutritional value. For instance, a salad with fermented garlic vinaigrette can be both flavorful and healthful.

The sustainability aspect of pickling and fermentation is another area of innovation. These methods are being used to reduce food waste by preserving seasonal produce and transforming lesser-used cuts of meat. This approach aligns with the growing interest in sustainable and responsible cooking practices.

In conclusion, pickling and fermentation is ripe with possibilities for flavor combinations and culinary innovations. These traditional methods, revered for their preserving qualities, are being reimagined in modern kitchens around the globe. From the fusion of different cultural flavors to exploring new ingredients and applications, pickling and fermentation offer an endless canvas for culinary creativity. As these techniques continue to gain popularity, they remind us of the rich heritage of our food traditions while inspiring contemporary gastronomic delights. The future of pickling and fermentation is not just about preserving food – it's about preserving heritage and innovating for a flavorful, healthful, and sustainable future.

Experimenting Safely with Your Own Creations

Experimentation with pickling and fermentation opens up a world of culinary possibilities, allowing both home cooks and professional chefs to explore new flavors, textures, and techniques. However, working with these methods involves more than just creativity; it also requires a keen understanding of the processes to ensure safety and success. This section delves into the principles of safe experimentation with pickling and fermentation, offering guidance on innovating while maintaining food safety and quality.

Pickling and fermentation have been used for centuries as methods to preserve food. Both processes inhibit the growth of harmful bacteria, but they achieve this in different ways. Pickling involves immersing foods in an acidic solution, usually vinegar-based, sometimes with added salt and spices. Fermentation, meanwhile, relies on the action of beneficial bacteria, yeasts, or molds to convert organic substances in the food into acids or alcohol. While these methods are effective at preserving food, improper techniques can lead to the growth of harmful microorganisms.

The first step in experimenting safely with pickling and fermentation is understanding the science behind these methods. For pickling, the acidity of the vinegar solution is crucial. The pH level must be sufficiently low (usually below 4.6) to prevent the growth of pathogens like Clostridium botulinum, the bacterium responsible for botulism. When creating pickling recipes, it's essential to use tested ratios of vinegar, water, and salt to avoid diluting the mixture with too much water or other non-acidic ingredients.

In fermentation, the key is creating an environment where beneficial bacteria can thrive while harmful ones cannot. This is typically achieved by controlling factors like temperature, salt concentration, and oxygen exposure. For example, lacto-fermentation, used in making sauerkraut or kimchi, requires an anaerobic (oxygen-free) environment, which is why the vegetables must be completely submerged in brine. The salt in the brine inhibits the growth of undesirable bacteria, allowing the lactobacillus bacteria naturally present on vegetables to proliferate and produce lactic acid.

When experimenting with new recipes, starting with small batches is advisable. This reduces waste in case the experiment doesn't turn out as expected and allows for more controlled testing of flavor development and safety. Documenting the ingredients, quantities, and steps taken during the process is also helpful for refining the recipe in future iterations.

One of the exciting aspects of experimenting with pickling and fermentation is the opportunity to play with different flavor combinations. Spices, herbs, and other flavorings can be added to pickling brines or fermentation jars to create unique profiles. For instance, adding juniper berries and caraway seeds to sauerkraut can give it a distinctively different flavor than the traditional recipe. Similarly, experimenting with various types of vinegar in pickling can result in different acidity levels and tastes.

However, experimentation should be conducted with caution. It's vital to use fresh and high-quality ingredients, as compromised ingredients can affect the safety and success of the fermentation or pickling process. Moreover, understanding the limitations and safety concerns of certain ingredients is crucial. For example, using honey in fermentation requires careful attention as it can contain harmful natural toxins in certain conditions.

Temperature control is another vital aspect of safe experimentation. Fermented foods require specific temperature ranges to ensure the proper growth of beneficial bacteria. Too warm, and the food can spoil; too cold, and the fermentation process may be inhibited.

Finally, awareness of the signs of successful and unsuccessful fermentation is essential. Good fermentation should result in a pleasant, tangy smell and taste, without mold or a slimy texture. Any signs of spoilage, such as an off odor, discoloration, or the presence of mold, mean that the food should be discarded.

In conclusion, experimenting with pickling and fermentation can be a delightful culinary adventure, full of creativity and flavor exploration opportunities. However, this experimentation must be underpinned by a sound understanding of the scientific principles behind these methods. By adhering to safety guidelines, using quality ingredients, and carefully monitoring the fermentation and pickling processes, enthusiasts can safely delve into the art of preservation, creating delicious and innovative foods that are both safe and satisfying to consume. This experimentation journey enriches the palate and connects us to the ancient traditions of food preservation, adapted for the modern culinary world.

CHAPTER VI

Long-Term Food Storage

Preparing Fermented and Pickled Foods for Storage

The art of preparing fermented and pickled foods for storage is a crucial aspect of preserving the flavors, textures, and nutritional benefits of these foods over time. This section explores the methods and principles behind storing fermented and pickled foods, highlighting the importance of proper techniques to ensure safety, quality, and longevity.

Fermentation and pickling are age-old practices used to extend the shelf life of food. While fermentation relies on the action of microorganisms to convert sugars into acids or alcohol, pickling typically involves immersing food in an acidic solution like vinegar. Both processes create an environment that inhibits the growth of harmful bacteria, but proper storage is key to maintaining their safety and quality.

For fermented foods, the primary concern in storage is maintaining the conditions that prevent the growth of undesirable microorganisms while retaining the beneficial properties of the fermentation. Once the desired level of fermentation is achieved, it's essential to slow down the process to prevent over-fermentation, which can lead to undesirable flavors or textures. This is typically done by lowering the temperature, as most fermentative microorganisms are less active in cooler conditions. Therefore, transferring fermented foods like sauerkraut, kimchi, or fermented dairy products to the refrigerator is a common practice.

When storing fermented foods, it's also crucial to ensure that they remain submerged in their liquid, whether it's brine or the juices released during fermentation. This anaerobic environment (free from oxygen) is necessary to keep the fermenting process stable and prevent the growth of mold and other spoilage organisms. For this reason, using appropriate containers is vital. Glass jars with tight-fitting lids are commonly used for home fermentation. In some cases, specialized fermentation vessels equipped with airlocks or water seals are employed to maintain an anaerobic environment while allowing gases produced during fermentation to escape.

On the other hand, the storage of pickled foods involves ensuring that the acidic environment created by the pickling process is maintained. Once pickled foods have achieved the desired flavor, they can be stored in their pickling liquid in airtight containers. Like fermented foods, pickled items should be refrigerated to slow down any further fermentation and preserve their texture and flavor.

The cleanliness of storage containers cannot be overstressed for both fermented and pickled foods. Containers should be sterilized to remove any bacteria that might contaminate the food. This can be done by boiling the jars and lids or using a dishwasher with a sterilizing cycle. This step is particularly crucial if the foods are intended for long-term storage.

Another consideration for storing fermented and pickled foods is the potential for continued fermentation, which can build up pressure in sealed containers. To avoid this, containers may need to be "burped" regularly - opening them to release any built-up gases. This is especially important in the first few days of storage when fermentation activity can still be relatively high.

Labeling is also an essential aspect of storing fermented and pickled foods. Labels should include the date of preparation and the ingredients used. This practice is not only beneficial for tracking the age of the product but also essential for identifying the contents, especially if you are experimenting with different recipes or flavor combinations.

The shelf life of fermented and pickled foods varies depending on the specific product, ingredients, and storage conditions. While many fermented foods can last for several months in the refrigerator, it's essential to use sensory cues (smell, taste, appearance) to assess their quality over time. Any signs of spoilage, such as off odors, colors, or flavors, indicate that the food should no longer be consumed.

In conclusion, preparing fermented and pickled foods for storage is a vital step in preserving these foods' safety, flavor, and nutritional value. Understanding and applying the principles of anaerobic storage, temperature control, container sterilization, and labeling can ensure that these delicious and healthful foods remain safe and enjoyable for extended periods. Whether a seasoned fermenter or a beginner, adhering to these storage practices is essential for anyone looking to explore the rich and varied world of fermented and pickled foods.

Proper Containers and Sealing Techniques

In the world of culinary preservation, the methods of fermentation and pickling have been cherished for their ability to extend the shelf life of food, while also enhancing flavor and nutritional value. An essential aspect of these processes lies in selecting proper containers and sealing techniques. This section delves into the intricacies of choosing the right containers and employing effective sealing methods for fermented and pickled foods, a practice critical to ensuring these products' safety, quality, and longevity.

Fermented and pickled foods require specific conditions to achieve the desired preservation and flavor development. The choice of container plays a pivotal role in this process. For fermentation, an anaerobic (oxygen-free) environment is essential for promoting the growth of beneficial bacteria and preventing the proliferation of harmful microorganisms. Glass jars, ceramic crocks, and food-grade plastic containers are commonly used for this purpose. Each of these materials has its advantages and considerations.

Glass jars are popular for small-batch fermentation and pickling. Their transparency allows for easy monitoring of the fermentation process, and they do not react with acids, ensuring that the flavor of the food remains unaltered. Mason jars and other similar glass containers with wide mouths are particularly favored for their accessibility and ease of cleaning. However, it is crucial to ensure that the jars are made of tempered glass to withstand pressure changes during fermentation.

Ceramic crocks are traditional for larger batches, especially for making sauerkraut, kimchi, and other vegetable ferments. They offer excellent insulation and maintain a stable temperature, which is beneficial for consistent fermentation. The porous nature of ceramic also allows for some air exchange, which can be advantageous for certain types of ferments. When choosing ceramic crocks, one must ensure they are lead-free and glazed with a non-reactive material.

Food-grade plastic containers are another option, particularly for large-volume fermentation. They are lightweight, durable, and relatively inexpensive. However, it is essential to use containers that are free from BPA and other chemicals that could leach into the food. The plastic should also be resistant to the acidic environment created during fermentation.

The sealing of containers is equally important in the fermentation and pickling process. An effective seal helps maintain the anaerobic conditions required for safe and successful fermentation and prevents contamination from external sources. In traditional pickling, the food is often submerged in a vinegar solution and can be stored in airtight containers once the pickling process is complete.

In fermentation, the requirement for an anaerobic environment often necessitates a more specialized sealing technique. One common method is to use a water-sealed crock with a moat-like structure around the rim that is filled with water. The lid sits within this moat, creating a seal that allows gases produced during fermentation to escape while preventing air from entering.

Airlock systems are another effective sealing method, particularly for jar fermentations. An airlock is a device that allows gases to escape from the jar without letting air in. This setup is beneficial for longer fermentation periods where the buildup of carbon dioxide needs to be managed safely.

Weighting down the contents of the container is also a crucial step in fermentation. This ensures that the food remains submerged in the brine and away from oxygen, which is essential to prevent the growth of mold and harmful bacteria. Glass weights, ceramic plates, or even clean, boiled stones can be used for this purpose.

When storing fermented and pickled foods, it is essential to keep the containers in a cool, dark place to slow down the fermentation process and preserve the flavors. Refrigeration is often recommended once the primary fermentation phase is complete.

In conclusion, selecting appropriate containers and applying effective sealing techniques are critical components in the art of fermenting and pickling foods.

The choice between glass, ceramic, and food-grade plastic depends on the fermentation scale, the ferment's specific requirements, and personal preferences. Similarly, sealing methods like water-sealed crocks, airlocks, and proper weighting play a pivotal role in creating the anaerobic conditions necessary for successful fermentation. By understanding and applying these principles, enthusiasts and professionals alike can ensure the safety, quality, and longevity of their fermented and pickled creations, continuing the rich tradition of these timeless food preservation methods.

Labeling and Organizing Your Preserved Food Stockpile

Preserving foods through techniques like pickling and fermentation is a time-honored tradition that has seen a resurgence in recent years. An essential aspect of preserving foods for future use is properly labeling and organizing the preserved stockpile. This section delves into the significance, methods, and strategies for labeling and organizing preserved food, ensuring that these culinary treasures are stored safely, efficiently, and in a way that maximizes their longevity and usability.

Labeling and organizing a preserved food stockpile are not merely practical tasks but are integral to these foods' safe and effective use. Proper labeling ensures that you can identify the contents of each jar or container at a glance, know when it was preserved, and understand any specific storage instructions. This practice is particularly crucial for fermented foods, which can continue to change over time. It is also an invaluable tool for tracking the shelf life of pickled items, which can vary depending on the ingredients and methods used.

The first step in effective labeling is to include the date of preservation. This information is critical for tracking how long the food has been stored and for using older items first, adhering to the "first in, first out" principle. The date can also be a guide to the fermentation process, especially for foods that continue to ferment while in storage, such as kimchi or sauerkraut.

In addition to the date, the label should clearly state the contents of the jar. This practice is critical when preserving a variety of similar-looking items, such as different types of pickles or fermented vegetables. Detailed labeling is also helpful for those with dietary restrictions or allergies, as it can include information about ingredients that may not be immediately apparent from the appearance of the food.

For those who like experimenting with different recipes and flavor combinations, the label can also include notes on the specific spices, herbs, or other flavorings used. This information can be invaluable for replicating a successful batch or adjusting future recipes based on past experiences.

The method of labeling should be practical and durable. Waterproof and smudge-proof labels are essential, as preserved foods will often be stored in environments where they might be exposed to moisture. Alternatively, one can use a permanent marker to write directly on the glass or lid of the container. Whichever method is chosen, the writing should be clear and legible.

Organizing the preserved food stockpile is equally essential. An effective organizational system allows for easy access to items and helps ensure that older foods are used first. This system can be based on the date of preservation, type of food, or frequency of use.

Storing similar items together is a practical approach. For example, all pickled vegetables might be placed on one shelf, while all fermented condiments are grouped on another. Within each category, items can be organized by the date of preservation, ensuring that older jars are at the front and used first.

Space considerations are another aspect of organization. Maximizing storage space while ensuring that each jar is easily accessible can require some planning. Utilizing shelving units effectively, employing safe stacking methods, and ensuring enough space between jars for air circulation are all crucial elements of good storage practice.

Temperature and light conditions are also essential factors in the storage of preserved foods. Most pickled and fermented foods benefit from being stored in a cool, dark place. This environment helps to slow down fermentation processes and preserve the flavor and texture of the food. A cellar, pantry, or even a dedicated space in a kitchen cupboard can serve as a suitable storage area.

In conclusion, labeling and organizing a preserved food stockpile is critical to home food preservation. Proper labeling provides essential information about the contents, preservation date, and any special notes related to the preparation or ingredients. Effective organization ensures that preserved foods are used on time, stored under optimal conditions, and are easily accessible when needed. These practices contribute to the safety and enjoyment of the preserved foods and reflect the care and attention that goes into the art of preservation. By adhering to these principles, one can maintain a well-organized, efficient, and safe preserved food stockpile, ready to be enjoyed throughout the year.

Shelf-Life Expectations

The shelf-life of fermented and pickled foods is a topic of significant interest for both novice and experienced practitioners of these ancient food preservation techniques. Understanding the longevity of these products is crucial for ensuring their safety, quality, and optimal enjoyment. This section explores the factors influencing the shelf-life of fermented and pickled foods, providing a comprehensive understanding of how long they can be stored and what affects their longevity.

Fermentation and pickling have been used for centuries as methods to preserve food. These processes extend the edible life of the produce and enhance their flavors and nutritional profiles. However, the shelf-life of these products can vary greatly depending on several factors, including the method of preservation, ingredients used, storage conditions, and the type of food being preserved.

Fermented foods, such as sauerkraut, kimchi, and yogurt, rely on the action of beneficial bacteria or yeasts to convert sugars and starches in food into acids, alcohol, or gases. This process naturally preserves the food and can extend its shelf life significantly. Generally, fermented foods can be stored for several months to a few years, but several factors can influence their longevity.

One of the primary factors affecting the shelf-life of fermented foods is the storage temperature. Fermented foods are best stored in cool, dark places, with refrigeration being ideal to slow down the fermentation process and prevent over-fermentation. Over-fermentation can lead to undesirable changes in flavor and texture, making the food less palatable or, in some cases, unsafe to eat.

The salt concentration in the fermentation brine also plays a critical role. Salt is a natural preservative that inhibits the growth of harmful bacteria. A higher salt concentration generally leads to longer shelf-life, but it can also affect the taste and texture of the final product.

Another factor is the acidity level, which is particularly important in preventing the growth of pathogens.

Fermented foods with a lower pH (more acidic) are less likely to harbor harmful bacteria and thus have a longer shelf-life.

The type of container used for storage can also impact the longevity of fermented foods. Air-tight containers are essential to create an anaerobic environment and prevent contamination. Glass jars with tight-fitting lids are commonly used, but it's necessary to ensure that the lids can release pressure that may build up due to continued fermentation.

In contrast, pickled foods are preserved primarily through an acidic solution, typically vinegar, and are often additionally flavored with various herbs and spices. Like fermented foods, pickled products can last for several months to years, depending on the preparation and storage method.

The shelf-life of pickled foods largely depends on the acidity of the vinegar solution used. Vinegar is a potent preservative, and a higher acidity level can extend the shelf-life of pickled foods. Most commercially prepared vinegars have an acidity level of around 5%, which is generally sufficient for preserving foods. Homemade vinegar, however, may have variable acidity levels, which can affect the preserving ability and, consequently, the shelf-life of the pickles.

Storage conditions are crucial for pickled foods as well. They should be stored in cool, dark places, and once opened, they should ideally be refrigerated to maintain their quality and prevent spoilage. The seal of the container is also essential; a proper seal ensures that the pickles remain submerged in the brine and are not exposed to air, which can lead to spoilage.

It's important to note that while fermentation and pickling can significantly extend the shelf-life of foods, these preserved items can still spoil. Signs of spoilage include an off smell, mold growth, or a change in texture. If spoilage is suspected, it is best to err on the side of caution and discard the food.

In conclusion, the shelf-life of fermented and pickled foods can vary greatly depending on various factors, including the method of preservation, the ingredients used, storage conditions, and the type of food. While these methods can preserve foods for several months to years, careful attention to storage conditions and signs of spoilage is essential. By understanding these factors, enthusiasts of fermentation and pickling can ensure that they safely enjoy their preserved foods for as long as possible.

CHAPTER VII

Incorporating Preserved Foods into Your Prepper Diet

Meal Planning with Pickled and Fermented Ingredients

Meal planning with pickled and fermented ingredients offers a unique opportunity to infuse dishes with complex flavors, enhance nutritional value, and bring diversity to everyday cooking. Incorporating these preserved ingredients into regular meal planning can elevate the culinary experience, catering to both health-conscious eaters and flavor enthusiasts. This section explores the various strategies and benefits of integrating pickled and fermented foods into meal planning.

Pickled and fermented foods have long been staples in many cultures worldwide, lauded for their preservation qualities and health benefits. These foods undergo processes that extend their shelf life and transform their flavors and nutritional profiles. Fermented foods like yogurt, kimchi, sauerkraut, and miso undergo a process where natural bacteria ferment the food, creating beneficial probiotics. On the other hand, pickled foods are preserved in an acidic solution like vinegar, often with added herbs and spices for flavor.

Integrating these ingredients into meal planning offers a myriad of benefits. Firstly, the probiotics in fermented foods contribute positively to gut health, aiding in digestion and the absorption of nutrients. These foods are also often rich in vitamins and antioxidants. With their tangy flavor profiles, pickled foods can add depth and zest to dishes, making them more appealing and satisfying.

When planning meals with pickled and fermented ingredients, balance is key. These ingredients tend to have intense flavors and should be paired thoughtfully with other meal components to create harmony on the plate. For example, the tanginess of sauerkraut can complement the richness of grilled sausages, while the sharpness of pickled onions can enhance the flavors of a hearty salad.

Breakfast offers an excellent opportunity to incorporate fermented foods. Yogurt can be served with granola and fresh fruit, or kefir can be blended into smoothies. Kimchi can be added to scrambled eggs or omelets for a savory option, providing a spicy kick to start the day.

Lunches can be enlivened with fermented and pickled ingredients as well. A simple sandwich can be transformed with the addition of pickled cucumbers or fermented chutney. Salads can be elevated with a scoop of tangy, fermented sauerkraut or a dressing made from yogurt. Light, pickled vegetables can serve as a crunchy, flavorful side that complements a variety of main dishes.

Dinner presents a canvas for creativity with these ingredients. Fermented miso paste can be used to marinate meats or incorporated into soups and stews for added umami flavor. Kimchi can be a side dish for grilled meats or stir-fried with vegetables for a quick, flavorful meal. Pickled vegetables can add brightness to rich dishes like stews or roasted meats.

Incorporating pickled and fermented foods into snacks and appetizers is also a great way to enjoy these ingredients. Olives, a classic fermented snack, can be served with cheese and crackers for a simple yet sophisticated appetizer. Pickled beets or carrots can be a refreshing and tangy snack on their own or added to a charcuterie board.

When meal planning with these ingredients, it's essential to consider their shelf life and storage. Most pickled and fermented foods should be stored in the refrigerator once opened, and it's advisable to use them within a reasonable period to enjoy their best quality and flavors.

Another aspect to consider is the sodium content in pickled foods and some fermented products. Those monitoring their salt intake should balance these foods with fresh, less sodium-heavy dishes throughout the week.

In conclusion, meal planning with pickled and fermented ingredients can be a delightful and healthful culinary journey. These foods not only bring diverse and robust flavors to dishes but also offer probiotics and essential nutrients beneficial for overall health. By thoughtfully integrating these ingredients into meals, one can enjoy a varied, delicious, and nutritionally rich diet. As the interest in traditional food preservation methods and gut health grows, pickled and fermented foods are valuable additions to modern meal planning, offering a taste of tradition in every bite.

Nutritional Benefits of Preserved Foods

Food preservation is a practice as ancient as civilization itself, originating out of necessity but evolving into a culinary art form. In recent times, the nutritional benefits of preserved foods, particularly those prepared through pickling and fermentation, have garnered significant attention. This section delves into the myriad of health benefits associated with preserved foods, shedding light on how these age-old methods contribute positively to modern diets.

Preserved foods, primarily those achieved through fermentation and pickling, offer a range of health benefits. Fermentation, one of the oldest food processing methods, is the metabolic process of converting carbohydrates to alcohol or organic acids using microorganisms—yeasts or bacteria—under anaerobic conditions. This process extends the shelf life of foods and enhances their nutritional value. Pickling, often involving the immersion of foods in an acidic solution such as vinegar, also serves to preserve while imparting unique flavors.

One of the most significant benefits of fermented foods is their probiotic content. Foods like yogurt, kefir, sauerkraut, kimchi, and miso are rich in beneficial bacteria that play a crucial role in gut health. These probiotics help balance the gut microbiome, which is vital for digestion, absorption of nutrients, and immune function. A healthy gut microbiome has been linked to numerous health benefits, including improved digestion, reduced risk of some chronic diseases, and even mental health benefits, such as reduced anxiety and improved mood.

Fermented foods are also known for their enhanced nutritional profiles. The fermentation process can increase the availability of vitamins and minerals in food. For example, the bioavailability of nutrients like B vitamins, particularly B12 in fermented dairy products, is increased. Fermented foods can also break down indigestible or harmful compounds, such as phytates in grains and legumes, enhancing overall nutrient absorption.

In addition to probiotics, fermented foods are often rich in enzymes, which aid in the breakdown and assimilation of nutrients. Enzymes play a crucial role in various bodily functions, including digestion, and the enzymes present in fermented foods can help improve digestive health.

Pickled foods, while not always fermented, also offer nutritional benefits. The primary preservation agent in pickling is acetic acid, commonly found in vinegar, which has been shown to have several health benefits. Acetic acid can help stabilize blood sugar levels, and some studies suggest that it may aid in weight loss and reduce blood pressure.

The spices and herbs commonly used in pickling, such as dill, garlic, and turmeric, can also contribute additional health benefits. These ingredients often have antioxidant and anti-inflammatory properties, contributing to the overall nutritional value of the pickled foods.

It is important to note, however, that pickled foods can be high in sodium, which can be a concern for individuals with hypertension or those on a sodium-restricted diet. As with any food, moderation is vital, and it is crucial to balance the intake of pickled foods with other lower-sodium options.

Another aspect of the nutritional value of preserved foods is their fiber content. Fermented foods like kimchi and sauerkraut are made from vegetables and, therefore, contain dietary fiber, which is essential for digestive health. Fiber aids in digestion, helps regulate blood sugar levels, and can contribute to a feeling of fullness, which may aid in weight management.

In conclusion, the nutritional benefits of preserved foods, especially those achieved through fermentation and pickling, are manifold. These foods provide probiotics for gut health, enhance nutrient availability, and offer additional health benefits through their enzyme and fiber content. While care should be taken with regard to sodium intake from pickled foods, incorporating these foods into a balanced diet can contribute positively to overall health and well-being. Preserved foods bring unique flavors to our plates and represent a harmony between ancient culinary practices and modern nutritional science, offering delicious and healthful options in our daily diet.

Creating Balanced Meals

Incorporating preserved foods into daily meals offers a delightful opportunity to add both nutrition and flavor. Fermented and pickled foods, with their rich history and health benefits, can be seamlessly integrated into a balanced diet. This section explores the art of creating balanced meals with preserved foods, highlighting how these ancient methods of food preservation can contribute to modern nutritional needs and culinary enjoyment.

The integration of preserved foods into regular meals involves more than just adding a tangy side of sauerkraut or a spicy bite of kimchi. It's about understanding the nutritional profiles of these foods and how they can complement other meal components. Preserved foods, particularly those that are fermented, are rich in probiotics, vitamins, and enzymes, and can enhance a meal's digestibility and nutritional uptake.

For a healthy and balanced approach, it's essential to consider the macronutrient composition - carbohydrates, proteins, and fats - and how preserved foods can fit into this framework. For instance, a breakfast bowl with yogurt, a fermented food rich in protein and probiotics, can be balanced with whole grain cereals and fresh fruits, providing fiber and essential vitamins. The tanginess of the yogurt complements the sweetness of the fruits, creating a harmonious and nutritious start to the day.

Lunch and dinner can be enriched with various fermented and pickled vegetables. A simple yet nourishing meal can consist of grilled chicken or tofu, brown rice or quinoa serving, and a side of kimchi or pickled beets. The fermented or pickled components add a burst of flavor and aid in digestion and absorption of nutrients from the meal. They introduce beneficial bacteria and add a dose of flavor without significantly increasing the meal's caloric content.

When creating salads, pickled vegetables like cucumbers, carrots, or red onions can add a delightful crunch and acidity, elevating the salad from a mere side dish to a culinary delight. Dressings made from yogurt or infused with fermented vinegar can also add probiotics and tanginess to the salad.

In the realm of snacks, fermented dairy products like kefir or cheese can be paired with whole grain crackers or vegetable sticks for a satisfying and healthful option. Pickled fruits can serve as a refreshing, low-calorie snack, perfect for mid-afternoon cravings.

It's essential to balance the distinct flavors of fermented and pickled foods with other meal components. More neutral-tasting foods like grains, lean proteins, or fresh vegetables best complement their bold flavors. This balance ensures that the meal is palatable and that the flavors of the individual components are harmoniously blended.

In addition to flavor, one must also consider the nutritional balance. Fermented and pickled foods can be high in sodium, so balancing these with low-sodium foods is essential. Similarly, if a meal includes a pickled item that is higher in sugar, like certain pickled fruits, balancing this with low-sugar foods in other parts of the meal is advisable.

Another aspect to consider in meal planning is the variety of preserved foods. The world of fermentation and pickling offers a vast array of options, from sauerkraut and pickled cucumbers to fermented soy products like tempeh and miso. Experimenting with different types of preserved foods can add diversity to the diet and provide a range of beneficial bacteria and nutrients.

In conclusion, incorporating preserved foods into meal planning offers a unique opportunity to enhance meals' nutritional value and flavor profile. The key to creating balanced meals with these foods lies in understanding their nutritional content, flavor profiles, and how they complement other meal components. By thoughtfully integrating fermented and pickled foods into a balanced diet, one can enjoy these foods' myriad health benefits while savoring their distinctive flavors. Preserved foods are not just a means of extending shelf life; they are a testament to the ingenuity of traditional food preparation methods and their place in a healthful, modern diet.

Cooking with Pickled and Fermented Ingredients

Cooking with pickled and fermented ingredients is a culinary adventure that adds depth, complexity, and a burst of flavor to everyday dishes. These ingredients, steeped in tradition and nurtured by time, bring more than just tanginess or zest to the table; they offer a nuanced palette of flavors that can transform the ordinary into the extraordinary. This section delves into the art of cooking with pickled and fermented ingredients, exploring the myriad ways these flavorful foods can be incorporated into various cuisines.

The roots of pickling and fermentation stretch back thousands of years, serving as methods to preserve food beyond its natural shelf life. Fermentation is a metabolic process in which natural bacteria and yeasts convert sugars and starches into alcohol or acids. On the other hand, pickling typically involves submerging foods in an acidic solution like vinegar, often with added salt and herbs or spices for flavor. Both methods extend the edible life of produce and infuse them with distinctive flavors – from the sharp bite of vinegar to the complex, slightly sour notes of fermentation.

Cooking with pickled ingredients can add brightness and a punch of flavor to dishes. Pickled cucumbers, onions, beets, and carrots are not just for side dishes or garnishes; they can also be integrated into main courses. For instance, pickled onions can be a vibrant addition to tacos or fajitas, offering a tangy contrast to the meat's richness. Pickled beets can be sliced and added to salads or sandwiches, bringing a touch of sweetness and acidity that balances well with leafy greens or creamy cheeses.

Fermented foods, rich in umami, can be the cornerstone of a dish or a subtle yet impactful ingredient. Sauerkraut can be used in a variety of ways beyond being a mere condiment for hot dogs. It can be warmed and served alongside pork or sausages, mixed into potato salads, or even included in savory pastries for an unexpected twist. With its spicy and tangy profile, Kimchi can be stir-fried with rice or vegetables, used as a topping for burgers, or incorporated into stews and soups to add depth and heat.

The incorporation of fermented soy products like miso and tempeh introduces not only flavor but also a significant nutritional boost to meals. Miso, a fermented soybean paste, can be used beyond soups; it makes for an excellent marinade for fish or chicken, imparting a salty, earthy flavor. Tempeh, a fermented soy product, can be stir-fried, grilled, or baked, serving as a hearty, protein-rich addition to meals.

One of the key aspects of cooking with pickled and fermented ingredients is balancing their strong flavors with other dish components. The acidity and saltiness of pickled foods need to be countered with milder, perhaps sweeter or creamier, elements. Similarly, the strong flavors of fermented foods should be complemented by other ingredients rather than overpowering them.

Another important consideration is the timing of adding these ingredients to the cooking process. Pickled ingredients are often best added towards the end of cooking or used as a finishing touch to maintain their crunch and vibrancy. Fermented ingredients, depending on their type, can be more versatile. Some, like miso, should be added at the end of cooking to preserve their probiotic qualities, while others, like sauerkraut or kimchi, can be cooked longer.

Cooking with pickled and fermented ingredients is not just about flavor; it also brings nutritional benefits. Fermented foods are known for their probiotic qualities, beneficial for gut health. They are also often rich in vitamins and enzymes. While sometimes high in sodium, pickled foods can offer vitamins from the preserved vegetables and the antioxidants typically present in the spices used in the pickling process.

In conclusion, the use of pickled and fermented ingredients in cooking is a celebration of flavor, tradition, and nutrition. With their complex flavors and health benefits, these ingredients offer endless possibilities to enhance and elevate dishes. From the tangy bite of pickled vegetables to the rich umami of fermented foods, they provide an array of creative and health-conscious cooking options. As more people seek to incorporate these traditional foods into modern diets, the art of cooking with pickled and fermented ingredients continues to evolve, offering a bridge between the past and the present, and between culinary heritage and contemporary tastes.

CHAPTER VIII

Health and Safety Considerations

Food Safety Guidelines

Food safety is paramount when it comes to preparing and consuming pickled and fermented foods. These ancient methods of food preservation, while beneficial in extending the shelf life of foods and enhancing their nutritional value, require careful handling to ensure they are safe to eat. This section discusses the food safety guidelines associated with pickled and fermented foods, covering the key considerations and best practices in their preparation, storage, and consumption.

Pickling and fermentation have been used for centuries as techniques to preserve various foods, ranging from vegetables and fruits to meats and dairy products. The processes involve creating conditions that favor the growth of beneficial microorganisms while inhibiting harmful ones. While generally safe, these methods can pose risks if not executed properly. Understanding and adhering to food safety guidelines is crucial to mitigate these risks.

Firstly, cleanliness is crucial in the preparation of pickled and fermented foods. This includes thoroughly washing hands, as well as sterilizing all equipment, utensils, and containers used in the process. Jars, lids, cutting boards, knives, and other equipment should be cleaned with hot, soapy water and then sterilized by boiling them for a specific time or using a dishwasher with a sterilizing cycle. This step is essential to prevent the introduction of harmful bacteria into the food.

For pickling, the use of a proper brine solution is essential for food safety. The brine, typically a mixture of vinegar, water, and salt, must be at the correct concentration to inhibit the growth of harmful bacteria, including Clostridium botulinum, which can cause botulism, a potentially fatal illness. Recipes should be followed precisely, and it's advisable to use recipes from reputable sources that have been tested for safety. The acidity of the vinegar used in pickling is also a critical factor; it should have an acetic acid concentration of at least 5% to ensure the food is preserved safely.

In fermentation, the key to safety is creating an anaerobic (oxygen-free) environment and maintaining the correct salt concentration in the brine. Vegetables and other foods must be fully submerged in the brine to prevent exposure to air, which can lead to the growth of mold and spoilage bacteria. Using weights or specialized fermentation lids can help submerge the food. It's also essential to monitor the temperature during fermentation; most fermented foods require a specific temperature range for the beneficial bacteria to thrive and for fermentation to occur safely.

Another critical aspect of food safety in pickling and fermentation is storing the finished product. Once pickled or fermented, foods should be stored properly to maintain their safety and quality. This generally involves refrigeration, which slows down fermentation and preserves the flavor and texture of the food. Fermented foods, in particular, can continue to ferment if left at room temperature, which may lead to over-fermentation and excess gas production, potentially causing jars to explode.

Regular inspection of pickled and fermented foods during storage is also essential. Signs of spoilage include an off smell, changes in color, the presence of mold, or a slimy texture. Any jars showing these signs should be discarded immediately. It's also essential to use clean utensils each time a portion of the food is removed from the jar to prevent contamination.

Labeling jars with the date of pickling or fermentation and the ingredients used can aid in monitoring the shelf life and safety of the foods. While many pickled and fermented foods have a long shelf life, they do not last indefinitely. Consuming them within a recommended time frame, based on the recipe and storage conditions, is advisable for both quality and safety.

For those new to pickling and fermentation, starting with simple recipes from reliable sources is a good way to ensure food safety. As experience and confidence grow, there may be more room for experimentation, but the basic principles of cleanliness, proper brine concentration, temperature control, and safe storage should always be followed.

In conclusion, while pickling and fermentation are effective and traditional methods of food preservation, they require careful attention to food safety guidelines. Cleanliness, precise recipe adherence, correct storage, and regular inspection are crucial to ensuring that these preserved foods are not only delicious and nutritious but also safe to consume. By following these guidelines, enthusiasts of pickled and fermented foods can enjoy the rich flavors and health benefits these foods offer while minimizing the risks associated with their preparation and storage.

Common Food Safety Mistakes to Avoid

Pickled and fermented foods have been a staple in diets worldwide for centuries, offering a unique blend of flavors and textures while providing numerous health benefits. These foods are not only delicious but also packed with probiotics and essential nutrients that promote gut health and overall well-being. However, despite their many advantages, people often make several common food safety mistakes when preparing, storing, and consuming pickled and fermented items. It is crucial to be aware of these errors to ensure the safety and quality of these delightful culinary creations.

One common mistake is improper preparation and handling of the ingredients used in pickling and fermentation. Whether you are pickling cucumbers, fermenting cabbage to make sauerkraut, or experimenting with other vegetables, it is essential to start with fresh, high-quality produce. Using vegetables that are overripe or have visible signs of spoilage can lead to foodborne illnesses and affect the final taste and texture of the product. Additionally, make sure to clean and sanitize all equipment and utensils thoroughly before use to prevent the growth of harmful bacteria.

Furthermore, the ratio of salt and water in the pickling or fermentation brine is critical. Many people make the mistake of either using too much or too little salt when preparing the brine. Too much salt can inhibit the growth of beneficial lactic acid bacteria, while too little salt can allow harmful microorganisms to flourish. Finding the right balance is essential to ensure a safe and successful fermentation process. Following a trusted recipe or guideline is recommended to determine the appropriate salt-to-water ratio for your specific pickling or fermenting project.

Another common mistake is neglecting proper hygiene during the fermentation process. Maintaining clean hands and utensils when handling the vegetables and brine is crucial. Contaminating the batch with dirty hands or utensils can introduce harmful bacteria that can spoil the food and even pose health risks to consumers. Regularly washing your hands and sterilizing utensils will help prevent contamination and ensure a safe fermentation environment.

Temperature control plays a significant role in the success of pickling and fermentation. Many individuals underestimate the importance of maintaining a consistent temperature during the process. The temperature should ideally be within a specific range, typically between 60°F to 75°F (15°C to 24°C), depending on the recipe. Extreme temperatures, whether too hot or cold, can slow down or halt the fermentation process. It is crucial to monitor the temperature and make necessary adjustments to create an ideal environment for the beneficial bacteria to thrive.

One of the most common food safety mistakes with pickled and fermented foods occurs during the storage phase. After the fermentation process is complete, it is essential to transfer the items to a suitable storage container and refrigerate them promptly. Many people overlook this step and leave their fermented products at room temperature for an extended period, thinking they will continue improving with time. However, this can lead to over-fermentation, spoilage, and even the production of harmful toxins. Proper storage in the refrigerator or another cool and dark place will help preserve the quality and safety of the food.

Moreover, failing to use clean and airtight containers for storage can also lead to issues. Oxygen exposure can promote the growth of mold and spoil the fermented foods. Therefore, choosing containers that can be sealed tightly to prevent air from entering and affecting the product is essential. Mason jars or fermentation crocks with airlock systems are commonly recommended for storing pickled and fermented items.

Additionally, many people make the mistake of neglecting to label and date their pickled and fermented foods. Proper labeling allows you to keep track of when each batch was made and ensures that you consume them within a reasonable timeframe. While fermented foods can have a long shelf life, knowing when they were prepared can help you determine their freshness and safety.

In conclusion, pickled and fermented foods are not only delicious but also provide numerous health benefits. However, to fully enjoy these culinary delights, avoiding common food safety mistakes is essential. Proper preparation, hygiene, salt-to-water ratio, temperature control, and storage practices are crucial for ensuring the safety and quality of pickled and fermented items. By following these guidelines, you can savor the unique flavors and reap the health benefits of these traditional foods without compromising your well-being.

Mold and Spoilage Detection

Pickled and fermented foods have a rich history and continue to be beloved for their unique flavors and health benefits. However, these foods are also susceptible to mold growth and spoilage, compromising their safety and quality. Detecting mold and spoilage in pickled and fermented foods is essential to ensure safe and enjoyable products are consumed. This section will explore the importance of mold and spoilage detection, the factors contributing to these issues, and the methods available to identify and prevent them.

Mold growth and spoilage in pickled and fermented foods are concerns that have been present for centuries. The natural microorganisms involved in the fermentation process are beneficial and contribute to the flavor and preservation of these foods. However, when unwanted microorganisms, such as molds and yeasts, contaminate the products, they can lead to off-flavors, odors, and even health risks. One common sign of mold growth is the presence of visible mold spots on the surface of the food.

These spots can vary in color, often appearing white, green, or black, and they may have a fuzzy or powdery texture.

Detecting mold and spoilage in pickled and fermented foods is crucial for several reasons. Firstly, it ensures the safety of consumers. Consuming spoiled or moldy foods can lead to foodborne illnesses, as molds can produce mycotoxins that are harmful to human health. Secondly, it preserves the quality of the product. Mold and spoilage can alter the food's taste, texture, and appearance, making it less appealing or even inedible. Lastly, it helps prevent economic losses for producers and manufacturers who rely on the successful production and sale of these products.

Several factors contribute to mold growth and spoilage in pickled and fermented foods. The most significant factor is improper handling and storage. If the food is not handled with clean hands and utensils or if it is stored inadequately, it becomes more susceptible to contamination. Oxygen exposure is another critical factor. Oxygen can promote mold growth, so it is essential to use airtight containers to store these foods. Additionally, temperature fluctuations and excessive humidity can create an environment conducive to mold and spoilage development. These factors highlight the need for vigilance in both home kitchens and commercial food production facilities.

Detection methods for mold and spoilage in pickled and fermented foods have evolved over time to meet the growing demand for food safety and quality. Visual inspection remains one of the simplest methods to look for signs of mold growth or spoilage on the food's surface. However, this method may not always be sufficient, as molds can grow beneath the surface or in less visible areas. Therefore, sensory evaluation, including taste and odor assessment, is another valuable tool in detecting spoilage. If the food has an off-putting smell or taste, it is likely spoiled and should not be consumed.

In recent years, technological advancements have introduced more sophisticated mold and spoilage detection methods. Microbiological testing involves taking samples from the food and culturing them in a laboratory to identify the presence of unwanted microorganisms. Molecular techniques, such as polymerase chain reaction (PCR), have also been employed to detect specific spoilage organisms and mycotoxins with high precision. These methods can provide accurate and rapid results, making them valuable tools for manufacturers and regulatory authorities to ensure food safety.

Preventing mold and spoilage in pickled and fermented foods begins with proper food handling and storage practices. Ensuring clean hands, utensils, and containers during preparation and fermentation can minimize the risk of contamination. Using airtight containers and vacuum sealing can help keep oxygen out and preserve the product's quality. Maintaining the correct temperature and humidity levels during storage is essential for preventing mold growth.

In conclusion, detecting mold and spoilage in pickled and fermented foods is critical to ensure both safety and quality. Mold growth and spoilage can compromise these traditional foods' flavor, appearance, and safety. Through visual inspection, sensory evaluation, and advanced testing methods, it is possible to identify and prevent these issues. Proper food handling and storage practices are essential in minimizing the risk of contamination and preserving the unique flavors and benefits of pickled and fermented foods. With the right knowledge and techniques, consumers and producers alike can confidently enjoy these culinary delights.

Food Allergies and Sensitivities

Pickled and fermented foods have long been enjoyed for their distinct flavors, preservation qualities, and potential health benefits. However, consuming these foods can pose challenges for some individuals due to food allergies or sensitivities. While pickled and fermented foods are generally safe for most people, it is crucial to understand the potential allergenic components and sensitivities associated with these products. In this section, we will explore the common allergens in pickled and fermented foods, the role of fermentation in reducing allergenicity, and how individuals with food allergies or sensitivities can enjoy these foods safely.

Common allergens found in pickled and fermented foods include ingredients such as soy, wheat, and fish. Soy sauce, a common component in many Asian-style pickled and fermented dishes, contains soy protein and can be problematic for individuals with soy allergies. Wheat-based products, like soy sauce or malt vinegar, can also be a source of concern for those with wheat allergies or celiac disease. Additionally, fish sauce and certain fermented fish products can be problematic for individuals with fish allergies.

However, it is essential to note that the fermentation process can sometimes reduce the allergenicity of certain ingredients. For example, soy sauce is often used in small quantities in pickling and fermentation, and the fermentation process can break down the soy proteins responsible for allergic reactions. This means that some individuals with soy allergies may tolerate fermented soy-based products like kimchi or miso better than unfermented soy products.

Similarly, wheat-based ingredients like soy sauce or malt vinegar undergo changes during fermentation that may render them less allergenic for some individuals with wheat allergies or sensitivities. Still, it is essential to exercise caution and consult with a healthcare professional if you have a known allergy or sensitivity to any of these ingredients. Sensitivity levels can vary among individuals, and what is safe for one person may not be safe for another.

It's worth mentioning that lacto-fermentation, a common method used in pickling and fermentation, involves the use of lactic acid bacteria to break down sugars and convert them into lactic acid. This process not only contributes to the tangy flavor of these foods but also helps preserve them. Lacto-fermentation can also enhance the digestibility of certain components, potentially making them easier to tolerate for individuals with sensitivities.

To enjoy pickled and fermented foods safely when you have known allergies or sensitivities, there are several strategies you can employ. First and foremost, read ingredient labels carefully. Manufacturers are often required to list common allergens in their products, making it easier for consumers to identify potential allergenic ingredients. If you have any doubts about the ingredients used in a particular pickled or fermented food, it is best to avoid it or contact the manufacturer for clarification.

If you enjoy making these foods at home, consider using alternative ingredients that are safe for your specific allergies or sensitivities. Many creative ways exist to substitute allergenic components without compromising flavor and quality. For example, you can use coconut aminos as a soy sauce substitute or gluten-free soy sauce for those with wheat allergies. Experimenting with different recipes and ingredient substitutions can open up a world of possibilities for individuals with dietary restrictions.

It's also important to communicate your food allergies or sensitivities when dining out or attending social gatherings where pickled and fermented foods may be served. Chefs and hosts are often willing to accommodate dietary needs and can provide alternative options that are safe for you to consume.

In conclusion, while pickled and fermented foods offer various flavors and potential health benefits, individuals with food allergies or sensitivities must be cautious. Common allergens like soy, wheat, and fish can be present in these foods, but fermentation may reduce their allergenicity for some individuals. Reading ingredient labels, making informed ingredient substitutions when preparing these foods at home, and communicating dietary restrictions when dining out are essential steps in safely enjoying pickled and fermented foods. With proper precautions and awareness, individuals with allergies or sensitivities can savor these culinary creations' unique tastes and benefits.

CHAPTER IX

Troubleshooting and Tips

Troubleshooting Guide for Pickling and Fermentation Issues

Pickling and fermentation are ancient food preservation techniques that have been practiced for centuries, yielding delicious and nutritious products. While these methods are generally straightforward, issues can sometimes arise, resulting in less-than-desirable outcomes. Whether you're experiencing problems with your homemade sauerkraut, kimchi, or pickles, understanding common issues and their solutions is essential for successful pickling and fermentation.

Mold growth is one of the most common problems encountered during pickling and fermentation. Mold can develop on the brine's surface or on the vegetables themselves, leading to off-flavors and potentially unsafe conditions. To address mold issues, it's crucial to maintain a clean and sanitized environment throughout the process. Start by using fresh, high-quality produce and ensuring that all equipment, utensils, and containers are thoroughly cleaned and sterilized. Additionally, submerge the vegetables fully in the brine to limit exposure to oxygen, as mold thrives in aerobic conditions. If you notice mold forming on the surface, carefully remove it with a small portion of the surrounding product and ensure the remaining vegetables are submerged. Adjust the salt concentration in the brine if necessary, as higher salt levels can inhibit mold growth.

Another common issue is a lack of fermentation activity, resulting in overly salty or underdeveloped flavors. If your pickled or fermented foods taste overly salty, it may be due to an incorrect salt-to-water ratio in the brine. To remedy this, refer to a trusted recipe to determine the appropriate salt concentration and adjust accordingly. On the other hand, if you experience a lack of fermentation activity and your vegetables remain crunchy instead of becoming pleasantly sour, it may be due to insufficient microbial activity. To promote fermentation, ensure that the vegetables are fresh, and the environment is at the correct temperature range for fermentation (typically between 60°F to 75°F or 15°C to 24°C). You can also try using a starter culture or whey from yogurt to introduce beneficial bacteria and jumpstart the fermentation process.

Over-fermentation is another challenge that can arise during pickling and fermentation. If your vegetables become excessively soft, mushy, or overly sour, it may be a sign of over-fermentation. To avoid this issue, monitor the fermentation process closely and taste the product regularly. Once the desired level of sourness is achieved, transfer the fermented food to the refrigerator to slow down the fermentation process and maintain the desired texture. Using airtight containers or fermentation crocks with airlock systems during storage can help preserve the product's quality and prevent over-fermentation.

Inconsistent or unpredictable results can also be frustrating for those experimenting with pickling and fermentation. The key to achieving consistent outcomes is to follow a trusted recipe and keep detailed records of your process. Measure the salt concentration, fermentation time, and environmental conditions meticulously, and make notes of any deviations or variations. By doing so, you can identify patterns and fine-tune your approach to achieve more predictable results in the future.

In some cases, gas buildup and pressure within fermentation containers can pose challenges. Gas buildup, often caused by the release of carbon dioxide during fermentation, can result in pressure build-up, potentially leading to container explosions or spills. To mitigate this risk, choose fermentation vessels that allow gas to escape, such as those with airlock systems or loosely sealed lids. Alternatively, "burp" the containers periodically by briefly opening them to release gas safely. Always exercise caution when handling pressurized containers to prevent accidents.

In conclusion, troubleshooting common pickling and fermentation issues requires a combination of good practices, careful monitoring, and adjustments along the way. Whether you're dealing with mold growth, excessive salinity, over-fermentation, inconsistent results, or gas buildup, understanding the root causes and implementing appropriate solutions will help you achieve successful and enjoyable pickled and fermented foods. As with any culinary endeavor, practice and patience are key to mastering the art of pickling and fermentation, leading to delicious and nutritious results you can enjoy and share with others.

Pro Tips and Secrets from Experienced Preppers

Preparing for unexpected emergencies and disasters is a practice that has gained significant attention in recent years. Those who engage in prepping, often referred to as preppers, understand the importance of self-reliance and readiness in times of crisis. While prepping can range from basic emergency planning to more advanced survivalist strategies, experienced preppers have valuable insights and tips to offer for individuals looking to become better prepared.

One of the first lessons from experienced preppers is the importance of prioritizing your needs. Prepping involves considering the essentials of survival: food, water, shelter, and security. Seasoned preppers emphasize the significance of building a well-rounded and diverse supply of these necessities. They recommend starting with a stockpile of non-perishable food items, such as canned goods, dried grains, and freeze-dried meals, which can sustain you and your family in times of food scarcity. Water storage and purification methods are equally crucial, as access to clean water can quickly become compromised during disasters. Preppers often advise having water filters, purification tablets, and a stockpile of bottled water. Additionally, prepping for shelter includes having a safe place to stay and the means to stay warm in cold climates or cool in hot ones. Blankets, tents, and weather-appropriate clothing should be part of your preparedness kit.

Security is another critical aspect of prepping that experienced individuals take seriously. While preppers hope never to encounter situations that require self-defense, they understand the importance of being prepared for such scenarios. Many preppers recommend learning self-defense skills and owning essential tools for personal security, such as firearms, pepper spray, and emergency whistles. However, it's necessary to emphasize responsible ownership and training in using such tools to ensure safety and effectiveness.

Effective communication is a key pro tip from experienced preppers. In times of crisis, staying informed and connected with loved ones is vital. Preppers often invest in two-way radios, satellite phones, and emergency communication devices that can operate independently of cellular networks. Establishing communication plans with family members and neighbors ensures that everyone knows how to contact each other and where to meet in case of separation.

Beyond the physical necessities, experienced preppers emphasize the significance of mental preparedness.

Maintaining a positive mindset, adaptability, and resilience is crucial during emergencies. Preppers often engage in mental preparedness exercises and practice scenarios to help them remain calm and make informed decisions under pressure. They also encourage building a strong support network within the prepping community and among like-minded individuals who can provide emotional support and share knowledge and resources.

Another valuable piece of advice from seasoned preppers is the importance of having a well-thought-out bug-out plan. A bug-out plan outlines the steps and locations you and your family should follow in case you need to evacuate your home quickly. Experienced preppers recommend having multiple bug-out locations, including both near and distant options, to account for different scenarios. The bug-out plan should include routes, transportation options, and essential supplies to grab in a hurry. Regularly reviewing and practicing your bug-out plan with your family ensures that everyone knows what to do when the time comes.

Resourcefulness and adaptability are qualities highly regarded by experienced preppers. They encourage learning practical skills such as first aid, foraging, hunting, and basic repair and maintenance. These skills enhance self-reliance and provide a valuable foundation for survival in various scenarios. Additionally, preppers often emphasize the importance of continually updating and rotating supplies to ensure their freshness and functionality. Regularly checking expiration dates on food and water, testing equipment, and replacing batteries in emergency devices are essential maintenance tasks for prepping.

Experienced preppers understand that preparedness is an ongoing process, and they encourage others to start small and gradually build their readiness over time. They emphasize the significance of progressively setting achievable goals and progressively acquiring knowledge and skills. Prepping is not about succumbing to fear but rather about empowerment and taking control of one's safety and well-being in uncertain times.

In conclusion, the insights and tips from experienced preppers offer valuable guidance for individuals looking to enhance their preparedness for emergencies and disasters. Prioritizing basic needs, focusing on security, emphasizing effective communication, maintaining a positive mindset, and having a well-thought-out bug-out plan are key aspects of prepping. Resourcefulness, adaptability, and a commitment to ongoing learning and maintenance are also vital for success in the world of preparedness. While prepping may seem daunting at first, taking gradual steps and incorporating these pro tips can help individuals and families become better prepared for whatever challenges the future may hold.

CONCLUSION

"Mastering Pickling & Fermentation: A Prepper's Guide to Preserving Food" is a comprehensive and invaluable resource for individuals seeking to enhance their food preservation skills and preparedness for uncertain times. Throughout the book, readers are presented with a wealth of knowledge, practical tips, and expert insights that equip them with the tools and techniques needed to pickle and ferment a variety of foods successfully.

The book begins by laying a solid foundation, explaining the principles and benefits of pickling and fermentation. It not only demystifies the processes involved but also highlights the health advantages and the ability to extend the shelf life of food through these methods. Clear explanations and step-by-step instructions empower readers to embark on their pickling and fermentation journey, whether they are beginners or experienced practitioners.

Its focus on prepper-specific considerations sets "Mastering Pickling & Fermentation" apart. It recognizes the importance of self-reliance and preparedness, offering insights into selecting the right ingredients, tools, and storage solutions for long-term food preservation. The book addresses common issues and challenges that preppers may encounter, providing troubleshooting guidance and pro tips from experienced individuals who have honed their skills in the art of preserving food.

Throughout the book, there is a palpable sense of the author's passion for pickling and fermentation, which is contagious. The recipes presented are diverse and delicious, ranging from classic dill pickles and sauerkraut to more adventurous creations like kimchi and fermented hot sauces. These recipes serve as both a source of inspiration and practical guidance, ensuring that readers can enjoy the fruits of their labor while bolstering their food security.

In conclusion, "Mastering Pickling & Fermentation: A Prepper's Guide to Preserving Food" is an exceptional resource that combines the art of food preservation with the wisdom of preparedness. It empowers readers to take control of their food supply, whether in times of crisis or as part of a sustainable, self-reliant lifestyle. With its comprehensive guidance and practical advice, this book is a must-read for anyone interested in pickling and fermentation's ancient and vital practices.

Thank you for buying and reading/ listening to our book. If you found this book useful/ helpful please take a few minutes and leave a review on the platform where you purchased our book. Your feedback matters greatly to us.

9 798869 175076